Continuing Ed

Continuing Ed

by Paul Schmidt

Continuing Ed

Published by Write-e-o Press
Lafayette, California

ISBN: 978-0-692-79821-8

Book design by Mark Shepard, www.shepgraphics.com
Cover art by Grant Wood

First Edition published October 2016

BOOK ONE

Continuing Ed

I t had been a few Easters since Ed had been back to where he grew up. The last time he'd been there, the whole family had gathered at Grandma and Grandpa Bumgartner's for Easter dinner, and all throughout the day Grandma Bumgartner had been making funny noises that resembled the sound of a helicopter drifting off into the distance - *FAFAFaFaFafafafafa*. Grandpa Bumgartner watched the grandkids play with their stuffed animals, and kept asking, "Hey, what's that sound? Those toys run on batteries?" missing the fact that it was Grandma in her declining state of what the family had been calling 'Uncle Al'. Ed's Aunt A had been so embarrassed. "For chrissakes, why doesn't he SHUT UP!" Of course, it would have been easier if the family had sought some insight and wisdom around Grandma B's condition, but hers was a situation nobody talked about. Nobody seemed to know how, and nobody made any attempts to learn how.

At the dinner table they teased Ed's brother Phil about how dirty his hands were. Phil owned a service station and spent much of his time beneath Mercurys and Chevys so that people could have reliable transportation. Phil, unruffled, simply replied, "I'm a workin' man." To which Grandma Bumgartner, who'd been silent all day except for *FAFAFaFaFafafafafa*, replied, "Yeah, and he works in bed too!" Everybody stopped eating, except for Grandpa, who hadn't hear her, and they all looked at Grandma B. Ed's aunt said under her breath, "Oh, for chrissakes!" Ed's mom turned red, and then somebody began talking about a book they'd read entitled *Beer Memorabilia*.

That was usually how things went where Ed came from, at least that was how he remembered them now. That was why he seldom went back home anymore - when he thought about it, his mind would move to events and scenarios that just made him roll his eyes and sigh. He'd decided that not much had changed in Wedlock, Iowa. And who ever heard of a town named Wedlock!? When Ed had first moved away and people would ask where he was from, he would tell them that he'd been in a horrible accident that had damaged his capacity to recall his childhood - anything but tell them he was from a place called Wedlock.

But Wedlock wasn't supposed to have been the name of the town. It was to have been named Wisteria City, but Mayor Myncrantz had been reading these racy novels where it was a common occurrence to have children born out of wedlock - and that word and image had stuck in his psyche.

The day they were to name the town, Mayor Myncrantz had spent a good part of the morning at the Tallcorn Tavern knocking back Sneaky Petes, so by the time he got up on the oak riser for the ceremony, his mind was drifting. He looked out at the crowd and noticed Mrs. Bathsheba - a 30-ish woman who looked like a Gibson Girl, certainly one of the most tantalizing expressions of womanhood in the town; and given the moment and Mayor Myncrantz's condition, her presence invited the Mayor's mind to the hope of scenes of imagined 'wedlock'. When he made the pronouncement, "And so, I hereby officially name this fair city … Wedlock!" there was a silence. People looked at each other without moving their heads, and then a confused ripple of applause rode through the congregation of people - a sound not unlike a small flock of flatulent geese. And, since Wedlock's inhabitants had little history questioning authority, people just figured, "I guess it was meant to be"; part of the same reason why nobody talked about Grandma Bumgartner's Alzheimer's Disease.

It was funny though, because there was a part of Wedlock that held a place in Ed's heart - a place where no stupid or terrible thing could touch the connection he had with his hometown. He'd lived many places, all of them more interesting and beautiful than Wedlock, but none of them felt like home - at least not in the same way, and that way was a way of wonder. That's probably what made it so difficult for Ed. He *WAS* from Wedlock. His roots were there, notwithstanding how little nourishment he felt they had received as he grew up, up, and away. He hadn't really wanted to go away - he had wanted to be *part of*, but no matter how hard he tried, the ceiling was always too low, the corridors too narrow. That reality made him sad, so he would remind himself of all of the Wedlock Ways that drove him nuts, and by the time he left, he'd convinced himself that his leaving was a triumph on the order of escaping *The Invasion of the Body Snatchers*.

As dusk was lying down across the pink and gold striated sky, Ed was pulling into the outskirts of Wedlock, out by Meinhard Messerschmidt's place. Meinhard Messerschmidt, whom everyone called Herm, had owned a hatchery in Wedlock. It was right on the edge of the downtown, at the bottom of the hill by the little popcorn stand that had appeared every summer of Ed's childhood, selling buttered popcorn and Bomb Pops - multi-coloured Popsicles that looked like Fruit Stripe gum on steroids, they were the Tiffany windows of the Popsicle world and a rare treat indeed.

Mr. Messerschmidt, which was how Ed's parents referred to him, was a happy fellow who wore a navy blue work uniform with 'Herm' embroidered on the right breast pocket. He wore thick-rimmed glasses that fit him perfectly, and he always walked as though he'd ridden his motorcycle for too long, which may very well have been the case. Mr. Messerschmidt had an old Indian motorcycle that had enough panache to be in a museum, and he always rode it wearing headgear that looked like a police cap without the lettering or badge.

Mr. Messerschmidt had made a little money in the 1960s during the 'chicken boom', as he liked to call it. Between the economy and his ads in *Leghorn Monthly*, he'd saved up enough money to buy his dream car - a '41 Lincoln. Mr. Messerschmidt had always admired them when he was a boy, but in those days there was no such thing as a car loan - what an extravagance! Nope, cars were bought with cash, and if you had a Lincoln or a Caddy it was because you had some serious dough. Mr. Messerschmidt kept that maroon baby spotless. One day when Ed was just learning how to drive and his interest in vehicles was peaking, Mr. Messerschmidt had the Lincoln out at the Dairy Queen down by the Wedlock Municipal Swimming Pool. He was showing it to Ed and was pointing out something just below the back window. Shaking his head he said, "See that? That's spider shit. I store it in the barn and I just can't keep the damn things away." Ed looked and looked, but he couldn't see anything, so he nodded in agreement. As Mr. Messerschmidt was pointing out the attack on his Lincoln, Ed noticed that portions of two of Mr. Messerschmidt's fingers were missing. Mr. Messerschmidt saw Ed observing his hand and said with a smile, "Woodworking accident. That's what happens when your apprentice is Jim Beam."

Country music held a big place in Mr. Messerschmidt's world as well. In the early days of the Grand Ole Opry, he and his buddies would rig up a radio antenna on his old Bel Air and go driving out in the countryside to the highest ground they could find so they'd be able to receive the signal all the way from Nashville. On a clear night it didn't sound too bad. They listened to Homer and Jethro, Roy Acuff, and Mr. Messerschmidt's favourite - Shot Jackson playing his dobro guitar. What a sound! He'd heard guys play dobro before, but nothing could touch the heartstrings of Mr. Messerschmidt's soul like Shot Jackson's dobro playing: singing and crying lines that made so much sense, evoking every range of emotion, from playful and smiling to romantic lament.

Yessir, Mr. Messerschmidt's deepest longing in life had been to play the dobro like Shot Jackson. His first Christmas bonus at the hatchery was matched in sum by his parents and they drove to Nashville to look in the pawnshops for an old dobro. Mr. Messerschmidt had heard that Shot preferred instruments made by Gretsch, so they looked high and low until they found a '39 Gretsch dobro, which came in a chipboard case scratched with the initials L. R., and which made the ride home with them in the backseat next to Mr. M.

Mr. Messerschmidt was never terribly gifted in the musical realm, but that didn't diminish his love for it. Ed got to see that first hand one time at a 4th of July celebration at the V. F. W. Hall in 1974. Shot Jackson himself had a band out of Nashville on a summer tour, and when Shot started to weave his dobro artistry, Mr. Messerschmidt cried like Mary at the cross.

At the end of the second set, Mr. Messerschmidt's wife Mildred was trying to get him to go introduce himself to Shot, but she may as well have asked him to strip naked and run into the church on Christmas Eve during the Candlelight Service - it was all too overwhelming for Mr. Messerschmidt. How can you just go introduce yourself to someone whose brilliance you've admired from a distance for nearly three decades? To Mr. Messerschmidt, Shot Jackson was like Rembrandt or Mozart! No. Mr. Messerschmidt was more than content to experience one of his life's finest moments from the darkness on the edge of a V. F. W. Hall in the heart of Iowa. Ed had watched it all, and the memory brought a smile to his face as he pulled into his parents' driveway.

Ed's parents, Mr. and Mrs. Anheiser. Mom and Dad. Frederick and Martha. Both of the porch lights were on, the front and the back, and Ed could see his folks through the big plate-glass windows in the front room - dad in his chair wearing his sunglasses so Martha wouldn't notice him falling asleep in front of the TV, and Martha on the floor drinking coffee and smoking her favourite cigarettes, Cancer Lights.

Ed turned off the engine and sat in the car surveying the portrait of the old homestead. The engine made ticking noises as it cooled off, the only accompaniment to his observations. He saw the fireplace where they used to hang their stockings every 6th of December, St. Nicholas Day: dark red rough bricks with hints of charring evidencing years of use, above which stood porcelain figurines of smiling cherubic females from the turn of the century that had belonged to Martha's Aunt Mae, all still arranged in the same fashion as when Ed had been brought home from the hospital after his birth. Aqua wingback chairs flanked the fireplace, and a plate bearing a stylized scene from *The Pickwick Papers* was hanging behind the one on the left. Ed recalled looking at that plate when he was eight years old, eating Bugles while watching The Three Stooges on *The Dr. Max Show*. He saw the ornately carved antique coffee table where he sat on Friday nights watching *The Wild Wild West* and *The Man From*

U.N.C.L.E., worlds that seemed to value exoticism and drama. It was all still there, all filled with his history.

He wondered now what that history would look like in the coming years. Frederick had been having some trouble with his heart - it looked like congestive heart failure, and there were the faintest hints of mild dementia. Ed knew that time would take its toll. He'd had the idea to make quarterly visits, and this was the first in the series of his plan. Ed walked though the front door, and Frederick popped out of his chair, "Weeelll, good to see you!" he said as he gave Ed a big authentic hug and an even bigger authentic smile. Frederick had such a happy smile. Martha greeted him with the usual, "Hi honey," and a kiss on the cheek that left Cranberry Red Revlon lipstick stuck in his beard. There were no new surprises on the front end of this conversation:

Frederick asked, "How long did it take you?"

"I'm not sure, Dad. I stopped a few times."

"Oh! How many miles did you get to the gallon?"

"I don't know, Dad."

"What were gas prices like in Illinois? Your mother and I came through there last year and around St. Charles it was pretty cheap!"

"Well, good for you, Dad." Ed thought that it was perhaps a prerequisite that everyone who lived in Wedlock needed to be gifted in the art of ephemera.

"Would you like some coffee?" asked Martha. Frederick and Martha drank three pots of Folgers coffee before retiring to bed, 365 days a year.

"No thanks mom. Got any Perrier and organic raspberry juice?" queried Ed.

"I might have some V8. How 'bout some Diet 7-Up and a braunschweiger sandwich? Daddy had one earlier."

"Naw, I'll just have some water."

The toughest part upon entering the place was the smell. That house was hermetically sealed twelve months a year - the only fresh air that got in was by mistake. Martha was afraid of pollen, even in January, so it was either the furnace or AC all year long. That might have been OK, but they'd both been smoking in the house for over half-a-century. The smell of burned cigarettes permeated everything: the carpet, the curtains, the upholstery, the plates, the silverware, even the sound of the doorbell. When packages would arrive from his folks, Ed knew who it was from without reading the label - the smell was the return address. One whiff said, Mr. and Mrs. Frederick Anheiser, 101 Home Blvd., Wedlock, IA.

After a little conversation, Ed told Frederick and Martha that he'd had a long day and wanted to head for bed. He took his big black garment bag up the stairs and plopped it on the summer-plaid couch in the room that used to be his. He looked around. Not much had changed. The couch was new, relatively speaking, and Frederick had set up an "office" since he retired from the University (ex-English prof.) - "forgotten but not gone" as Frederick was wont to say. The paneling was still up - the handy neighbor who'd worked at the Carnation plant had done it in seven straight summer evenings years ago. It looked the same.

Ed bent down and looked out the window - the window he had prayed at when he was a boy, the window he'd looked out during Christmas vacation nights as smoke rolled out of the neighbor's white stucco chimney and the lights from across the river shone through the sparkling air, clear and sharp like diamond star splinters. He had spent hours at that window. For a moment he saw in it the reflection of KROX Kommix Klassix, a series of old movies beamed out of Rochester, Minnesota, onto the old Motorola - the first time he'd ever seen the Marx Brothers and W. C. Fields, all by himself, alone in his room in the deep mid-winter. There was a vast word-transcendent feeling of sadness that washed over him - a sadness that had a beauty, but a sadness nonetheless. So much came flooding back and he didn't know what it was. His heart felt like Neil Young's voice.

Dawn came early for Ed. It was just a bit after 7 and he rolled over to see the old neighborhood in the daylight. The long, sloping hill that Ed always thought looked like the hill he sang about in *There Is a Green Hill Far Away* greeted him with the memory of sliding down it in every season. The Schildersteins had lived there when Ed was a slider, and Mr. Schilderstein would get especially angry in the springtime for he never gave up hope of having a "lawn to be proud of," but it never happened until all of the neighborhood kids got to high school, and by then the Schildersteins had moved into an assisted-living community.

Across the street was where Florence and George had lived - an elderly couple in a canary-yellow bungalow that had an unusual architectural feature - attached garage. Florence had MS and Ed had only ever known her in her wheelchair. He would visit with her on Saturday mornings, when the weather permitted, as she wheeled her way up and down the front sidewalk. She was not pretty on the outside, but on the inside she was young and smart and personable. Ed smiled and raised his eyebrows at the memory.

He listened for Frederick and Martha, but the house was dead silent. They didn't usually stir much before 9, so Ed thought it might be fun to go to breakfast somewhere in Wedlock. He threw on some fresh clothes and headed out. When he got to the bottom of the hill he looked for Shep's - the old service station run by Hezzie and Oak that he and two of his neighborhood friends, Annette and Danny, would visit on the weekends to buy candy. It was close enough to home that they could walk, but far enough away that it felt like a little adventure. With money left over, they could get five or six pieces of red and green licorice, a Slo Poke, some wax lips, a bag of Gold Nugget gum, some Beatles cards, and a bottle of pop - if Hezzie and Oak were in good enough moods to not make them pay the deposit. They'd take their loot over to the old Lincoln School playground and then slip through an opening in the wall of the Spahn & Rose Lumber Company storage barn to visit and consume amidst the plywood and spruce. Those were good days. But Shep's was long gone, and in its place was a parking lot for the new bank with a sign that lit up time and temperature. Ed hesitated for a minute, sighed, and then engaged the turn signal with his middle finger.

He turned right and headed up Main Street. As he was crossing the bridge that joined the two halves of Wedlock, more distant musings stepped forward. He could see the blazing frozen riverscape in the darkness of the frigid days after Christmas vacation when he and Lyle Doolittle got up in the deep-harshness of winter to walk to basketball practice at the Junior High, the Victorian fortress inhabited by lockers and cement. It was below zero, the burning ice-wind whipped them with a yowl, and both he and Lyle wondered why they were doing it. They thought, "Why are we braving this horrendous weather and depriving ourselves of warmth and rest only to supplant it with coach Spermbach yelling at us?" But neither of them ever spoke about it - it was too vulnerable.

The vision quickly shifted to the heat of that following summer and the time he went fishing off the bridge with his friend Tom Terrific and his mighty dog Manfred. They caught thirty-three bullheads, and had no idea what to do with them. It was the same place he had stood by himself throwing rocks at the dam on an overcast Good Friday afternoon, pondering the meaning of "sacrifice for the sake of love." He recalled the church service when one of the pastors put ashes on his forehead and said, "Remember that you are dust, and to dust you shall return." Ed had thought at the time that no, he wasn't dust, he was a beloved child of God, but nobody had asked him what he thought about it. When they got back to the pews, Phil passed him a note that read, "If we are dust, then who is living on our furniture?"

All of these things came in an instant, like the sound of a light bulb burning out, and it touched something in him. He was drawn back to the moment when he stopped at the traffic light and chuckled at the "Psychedelic State" sticker on the back window of the light green van ahead of him; but as he looked over to his left he noticed the huge old turquoise house by the Chrysler dealership, and then he saw it as it had been, and then he saw Her. Juliette Jacquette. It had been Juliette Jacquette's house. Oh God! Juliette Jacquette! Juliette Jacquette!

He turned off Main Street and parked across from the house. His mouth was open and his eyes widened - the memories were as fresh as lilacs are sweet. Juliette Jacquette had been the sort of girl-woman whose smile spread like a butterfly in the lawn of desire. Excitement hung around her like an atmosphere. She'd a laugh like a rose. Surely, she was one for whom Song of Solomon had been written.

She was not the culture's quintessential beauty, but she was one of the most exemplary expressions of womanhood that Ed had ever experienced. He adored her physical attributes - ice-blue eyes, porcelain skin, three feet of raven-coloured hair, proportions of a goddess, scent of nectar; but what really roped his heart was her *her-ness*. She was femininity in all of its splendour - intuitive, intelligent, kind, aware, humorous, creative, and passionate. As far as the fruits of the spirit went, her basket was full.

She and Ed had been fast friends since grade school, and by the time they got to high school their friendship had not diminished, but it had been stilted by their mutual inability to make the growing-up transition. Ed was sure that they had loved one another as deeply as any two people could love, but nobody had helped them navigate the waters of something so profound. They couldn't seem to weave the romance piece into their friendship - there were so few models of it. The movies they saw always showed the sexes manipulating one another, or desiring one another as one would desire a victory in a sport. Ed's friends talked about females as objects to give them pleasure, and that didn't feel right to him. Certainly he was gifted with the beautiful primal desires of any healthy heterosexual male, but they always felt incomplete without the context of some true and whole relationship. Of course, Ed couldn't have worded it so at the time, but his intuition had enlightened that wordless truth nonetheless. No, he and Juliette had entered into the sea of adult relationships upon the ship of confusion - a vessel that took them to ports in places where they were no longer together.

Ed let the tears fall there in the car - their saltiness was loud and as bitter as the memory. He reached for his heart, for he felt it breaking all over again. Silence. Then anger. What he would have given for some clarity! How can they send you through school and never teach you anything about what you really need - HOW TO DO RELATIONSHIPS! It was profound in its absurdity! Socialized orthodox insanity! A system so filled with left-brain linear bullshit! A system so imbibed with competition, winning, dominance and control! A system so antithetical to the human condition - a still-thriving horror of the Post-Enlightenment! Surely it was one of the modern triumphs of evil!

Surely, it was.

That was one of those experiences that reminded him of why he left Wedlock. It was Wedlock's fault, or so he had thought for the longest time.

After his heart quit racing he started up the car and aimed it towards the edge of town where the new Walmart had been erected. Ed was not a "chain" guy - he'd rather pay a little bit more money and have a limited selection in exchange for knowing the store owner. But now that he didn't know anybody, and Bertha's Diner had been turned into an H&R Block office, he figured that the restaurant at the Walmart made as much sense as anywhere else. And after his Juliette Jacquette memory, he was bound and determined not to enjoy himself.

After a lonely breakfast of hefty-ridden Midwestern fare and four cups of legally addictive drugs that tasted like molten cigarettes, he decided that as long as he was at Walmart he'd pick up another liter of Diet 7-Up for Martha. On his way out through the parking lot he noticed the cars - they were different than the ones in the city. These cars were all American makes, and many of them were older, and in colours that seemed uninterested in beauty. Then he remembered Kermit Grunder's car.

Ed had been about eight or nine when he first experienced Kermit Grunder's Mammoth-Mobile. It was a dark purple Hudson covered with white polka dots and wired up with radio antennae on all four corners that made it resemble a cross between a mobile by Alexander Calder and a pregnant ladybug on LSD. "Hey Look - it's Kermit!" shouted Phil when the visage of Kermit's machine swooshed by. Ed had been speechless - most people were the first time they saw Kermit's car.

Kermit Grunder lived in the country all by himself - Frederick liked to call him "Kermit the Hermit." Kermit's wife had died of a flu when he was serving in North Africa during WWII and he'd never remarried. After he came back from the war, Kermit figured there would be a lot of new building going on, so he speculated that they'd need to have facilities to accommodate the construction workers. Kermit opened a business that was one of the earliest incarnations of what were later referred to as Porta-Potty Services. Kermit called his *Grunder's Grunters*, and his card read: *"We're Number One AND Number Two - And That's No Shit!"* He had a truck with his picture on each mud-flap and a bumper sticker that read *Be Nice to Crickets*.

One time Kermit went to a church council meeting when they were deciding what kind of boiler to put into the Parish Hall, and after Kermit had stated his position, Marvin Mabon, a member of the Property Committee, agreed with him. Kermit stood up and yelled, "See, that's the problem around here! Nobody ever listens to me!" Marvin looked at him for a moment and said, "Kermit, I just agreed with you." Kermit looked at Marvin, then at Pastor Scheister, and as he sat down, he said, "Oh."

That was Kermit - a guy with a sewage business and a confused disposition that flew its flag high in the theatre of his transportation.

But as Ed reflected, he knew he never really knew Kermit - he knew Kermit in the same way he thought most people knew Kermit, which was that they didn't really know him, and that they didn't really know that they didn't really know him. Ed wasn't so sure anyone really knew anyone else in Wedlock. When he was younger, Ed had theorized that most of Wedlock suffered from a malady endemic and indigenous to the area - called it F. I. S. - Frightened Iowa Syndrome - a genetic disease that prevented people from evolving, that blocked any real communication, and that left intimacy as a word in the dictionary rather than an experience that anybody ever really had or cared about. And if they ever needed any help engaging the symptoms of F. I. S., there were two manuals to refer to: *Fear is Your Friend*, and *How to Be Miserable Even When Things Are Going Pretty Good*. And there was the annual F. I. S. convention, AngstFest. It had been a clever theory on Ed's part, but it was snarky, and it never left him experiencing much joy.

It wasn't even ten o'clock and Ed already had a taxing day under his belt. He came back home to discover Frederick and Martha sitting across from one another at the table in the back room - Martha looking out the back window holding a Cancer Light and drinking coffee, and Frederick underlining things in his daybook with a red felt-tipped pen and a ruler.

"Hey, where ya been?" inquired Frederick, with a smile as broad and cheery as a Clement Moore Santa.

"Oh, I got up early and thought I'd get some Diet 7-Up. Where do you want it mom?"

Martha, half asleep, replied, "Just put it there, honey," motioning to the white wicker planter where sundry other liters of Diet 7-Up were napping.

They visited for awhile when the phone rang and Martha got up to answer it. When Martha left the room, Frederick said to Ed, "She just can't let the phone ring, she always has to answer it! How important could it be? I never answer the phone. Do you answer the phone at your house?" Ed tried to explain some of the more basic technological advances that included the option of having a device that would allow one to receive a message, but it all sounded way too complex to Frederick.

Frederick asked, "Hey, do you ever see that fellow Frank?" Frederick liked to ask Ed about people whom Ed had met when he'd first moved to Chicago fifteen years earlier - people whom Ed had told his folks about because they were nothing like anyone from Wedlock - people whom Ed hadn't seen in over a decade.

There was the fellow who had been a lounge singer turned coffee importer named Frank Sumatra, whose best man at his wedding had been a hit man for Al Capone. Frank and his best man, Tommy Jewel, had once hijacked a Kroger truck and taken it to an ethnic neighborhood down by the stockyards, broken open the lock with an ax, and let people take what they needed. Frederick liked that story. So did Ed. Then there was Eliot Finesse, the coiffeur who was smitten with detective novels and ran a clothing store called The Dandy Lion. There were two widowed sisters who ran a magic shop and rented old horror movies - Doris Karloff and Stella Lugosi; and the bodybuilder/pasta salesman, Al Dente. And then there was Tab Lloyd, a writer for *The Chicago Times* gossip column; and the marathon runner who owned a travel agency, Moe Mentum.

To Frederick, these people were like Martians, yet they intrigued him to no end. He'd smiled when Ed told him their stories, laughed at the extremes to which they lived their lives, and gloried in the colorfulness with which they painted the world - yet their actions were nothing that Frederick would have ever considered for himself. Maybe that was why they were so intriguing to him. Maybe that was why Ed liked to tell the stories.

"I don't really see Frank anymore, Dad. He had to put his wife into a nursing home and sell his shop. I haven't really seen him in years."

"That's too bad," said Frederick, "About his wife I mean, and that you haven't kept in touch."

Ed heard that. It *was* too bad, on both accounts. Ed felt the vacancy. He asked Frederick, "Hey, what about Hudson?"

Hudson Voray was a colleague of Frederick's in the English Department at the University of Wedlock, and a truly amazing fellow. He had grown up in the rural South with sharecropper parents who'd transplanted him from place to place. He'd retreated into books and become fascinated with Walt Whitman's travels and reflections, probably because he could relate. Hudson's insights were Wisdom incarnate - sharp, poetic, and grounded with timeless expanse. Thoreau had nothing on this guy.

Ed remembered when Hudson's first book, *Vexation and*

Vomit, came out - a collection of poems, short stories, and essays that was filled with passion and depth - things that were not necessarily considered features at the school or in the town.

Every autumn Hudson would host Voray's Forays, a conference for inventive writers, typically capped-off by Hudson reciting one of his wildest works. Hudson was compassionate and funny, and always filled with questions that nobody in the world could answer. He'd enter the faculty lounge on the 3rd of July and lead with, "How could a nation founded on freedom have a first president who kept slaves!?" Or when he'd get his tax refund he'd rant and rave about the fact that the bank actually cashed it - "How can they cash a check from a source that the entire world knows is trillions of dollars in debt!?" Or, right before Christmas vacation it would be, "If the whole notion of Christianity is based upon the concept of a God who is loving, how could people who claim that they're Christians be exclusive to people who've been given a different understanding of the Divine!?"

Ed loved the mystery - the who-knows-ness of it all. But these kinds of things often bewildered Frederick. He wasn't that much of an explorer - he was more at peace with the Classics, and pretty content with what had passed. Yet, he was a steadfast friend to Hudson - always invited him over for parties, always took him to lunch on his birthday, and always sent him a card at the holidays.

In response to Ed's question, Frederick dropped his face, looked out the back window towards the old stone birdbath, and said, "He died last year. Your mother and I found out about it when we got our Christmas card back - it came in an envelope with a note from his daughter. After he didn't get tenure, he left the University to take a position as editor-in-chief of some poetry journal in Connecticut. Apparently, the stress of funding wore him down to where he didn't write anymore. Personally, I think he died of a broken heart."

Both Frederick and Ed were silent - probably the same way in which Theo was silent when he found out that Vincent had been unable to endure the world. The analogies were similar and thorough.

Martha walked back into the room, "Who died?"

"Oh, I was just telling Ed about Hudson."

"He was a character, but he had a good heart," said Martha (as though having "character" was a flaw).

Ed was affected. Hudson was one of his role models - someone who had really paid attention to his inner voice, notwithstanding the stilting surroundings - someone who was authentic and soulful amidst a sea of weak soup. "That makes me sad," said Ed, to no one in particular.

"Hey, how about some lunch - it's almost 11:30," chimed Frederick. It was one of the stock pathways in the Anheiser household, as though a sign in each room read, *In Case of Real Moments, Offer Food*.

They visited awhile longer, Ed listening to Frederick's accountings of other of Frederick's former colleagues, like Ulysses S. Grant. Ed had always sensed that Grant was functionally nuts, a trait that was intriguing if not confusing. When one spoke to Grant, his eyes turned to saucers, and the longer the conversation lasted, the further away from it Grant became.

Ed asked if Willem Mudde might be coming back over from Europe for another poetry reading. Frederick had met him while on a Fulbright in Holland in the late '50s, and they had remained colleagues and true friends ever since. Ed remembered polishing Mr. Mudde's shoes - ancient oxfords with badly worn soles and a finish that would not shine no matter how many times Ed polished them. Ed remembered looking at them, observing the cracks, the wear. They looked deceased, but they were Mr. Mudde's only pair. Frederick had told Ed that during WWII the Nazis chased Mr. Mudde through the streets of Holland, and only under the cover of night had he gotten away and hidden. Despite his history, or perhaps because of it, he always wore a grateful smile.

They visited a bit longer, but soon Ed felt as though he needed a nap. The news about Hudson had wounded him sharply and he needed some time to recover. He excused himself and went upstairs to lie on the plaid couch. What was he going to do? He hadn't been back fifteen hours and already Ed was unbalanced - emotionally and spiritually fried. But, come to think of it, that was usually how it had been every time he'd come home. Things hit Ed like a hurricane - he'd always been a sentient person and felt things deeply, and with all things Wedlock it was as though they went into his marrow. Perhaps it was because things there had such a rootedness - they had been so primary to his being.

The next day, Frederick and Ed spent the entire time sitting in the back room talking and drinking coffee. Martha usually only lasted about twenty minutes, but "the boys" could sit there from breakfast, through lunch and dinner, and still be visiting when it was time for Frederick to watch the late news at 10 o'clock.

They had conversations they'd had before - the first of which was usually the one about education. They bemoaned how higher education had diminished into training for competitiveness. They were completely baffled by those who had forgotten that the foundation of ancient education had been based upon first-hand experience in the marketplace, the theatre, and in religious celebration. True knowledge was about discovery. Ed always liked to repeat, "Heck, Socrates met people in the street, at dinner parties, after festivals, not at some Athenian Harvard!" They both knew that the Classical philosophers would've abhorred being turned into monuments - authentic human becoming was to be about reflection and knowledge born out of contact with the real world, aimed at the singular truth of enlivening the mind - the mind of one's heart.

They believed in what they liked to call *Slow Knowledge*. One time during this familiar discussion when they were high on Folgers (orbiting might be an even more descriptive moniker), they worked out a definition for *Slow Knowledge* that they pondered committing to a T-shirt; it went: *Slow Knowledge is that which is bred from thoroughness and patience, signified by harmony, awareness, and patterns that give our lives aesthetic, spiritual, and social meaning.* It was a great definition, but when they drew some sketches, it didn't look so good on the T-shirt.

When they really got going they liked to talk about education as a dialogue with ideas, reality, society around us, and those who had gone before. After awhile they weren't even looking at each other - they were just expounding into space, looking towards the tops of windows, talking to no one. Much truth was espoused, but little activity ever ensued.

Sometimes they inadvertently decided to get nasty, going nutty pummeling the administration at the University of Wedlock, a beating that came in response to their own experiences there - "Ants addicted to certitude! Blurring the glow of truth! Why they're constantly missing the essence of the humanities as a foundation for thinking, for learning to reflect! They're just imbibed with technical training, training which by its very nature is sure to become obsolete!"

Yikes!

Though accurate in their fervour, their accuracy did not bring them peace; in fact, it often made them crabby. There was much laughter, but too much of it was built upon sarcasm and cynicism, and by the end of the day, with their nerve endings misfiring with the ferocity of one of Field Marshall Rommel's divisions, they felt bloated with the rotted fruits of their musings, caffeine, and all things sedentary. Fatigued. Stalled. When the caffeine wore off they'd take some Tums and go to bed with a spectre of sour as their goodnight kiss.

But then there were the discussions that were softer and more reflective. Ed and Frederick both took comfort in the story of the Christ figure - the outlaw who was despised by the rich and the religious, the one who loathed all sham and deceit, the one whose singular message had been Love, and the belief that all of life was about Loving One Another - that for which all else was but preparation. Their conversations did indeed bring all of their understandings of life into focus, and those conversations were secretly one another's favourites.

There was the discussion about the gay issue, which Frederick was relatively liberal about. Martha was homophobic so Frederick didn't get much of a chance to talk to anyone who thought much about it. It was odd though - Martha would get scarlet with indignation when the topic was broached, and then entertain visiting gay poets as though they were royalty.

Frederick liked to talk about cars and money, and then complain that all of the people he knew anymore just wanted to talk about cars and money.

As Ed lay in bed after a day of all of that, a moment of Light said, "You can't do your days like this, you'll never survive." He knew it was Truth inviting him back to his design. Ed fell asleep trying to pay attention.

Phys. Ed.

The lighting of the world came as the sunlight poured through the east windows like the fresh iridescent amber of young cellos. Ed awakened to KWWI fuzzily narrating a soybean report from the old G.E. radio/alarm clock Phil had bought when his deal for a used motor scooter fell through. Ed listened to the voice, and when he heard the station identify itself - "This is KWWI with an eye out for you!" - he recalled his trip to the KWWI radio and TV studios. Ed's Confirmation class had taken a tour of Iowa Falls landmarks, the first being a visit to the Massey Ferguson factory. The experience of the foundry had left Ed startled - the blinding noise, molten metals pouring from buckets the size of Buicks creating a stench beyond the endurable. Ed thought it was a reenactment of Sheol - perhaps the real reason why a tractor factory had been put on the Confirmation agenda. When one of the chaperons asked the tour guide about the effect of the working conditions on the workers' mental health and respiratory systems, the guide looked at the questioner with steel eyes and laconic snap and replied, "If you want tractors, this is what it takes." End of conversation.

The confirmands toured the TV studios of KWWI, channel 7 on your TV dial, local programming that featured *Floyd Stufflebeam's Iowa Jubilee Show* with Uncle Ernie Blank on the vocals, sponsored by Massey Ferguson. Theme song:

When a man works the land he's a man's kind of man
He's a doer, not a talker, he's a cultivatin' man

He's a get up early, keep 'em rollin' Massey Ferguson
kind of a man
*He's got power at his fingertips (*drum fill*)*
A farm well run
He depends on Massey Ferguson to get the job well done
Well Done!

It was the only local music on TV, so Ed used to watch as Floyd played the accordion, his daughter Dottie played the saxophone, Uncle Ernie played the drums and sang, and the occasional guest appeared to tell jokes or do magic tricks. Ed hadn't really liked the show, but he had liked the idea of local musicians appearing on television. It was, of course, just filler for the Massey Ferguson advertisement in the same way that all of TV is just filler for the commercials, but Ed didn't realize that until much later.

During the tour, Ed got to peek through a window into one of the studios where they were taping *KWWI All-Star Wrestling*. There in full three-dimensional audacity were the stars of the weekly two-dimensional organized violence broadcast that graced the viewing audience of the greater Iowa Falls area: Bobby Shane, Bearcat Wright, and The Viking. Bobby was a boyishly-cute 20-something fellow who was respectful and wrestled by the rules - a good guy. Bearcat Wright was a large man of African descent with the physique of a Greek god, also a good guy. When Bearcat got punched (illegal) he'd respond with a slap (legal). The Viking was a thick man in his forties with white hair and a pointy beard who would put opponents in a headlock, turn them away from the ref, and then swing his hitch-hiking-ready thumb into their throats, the effect being writhing and convulsing on the part of the headlocked one, and victory for The Viking. Ed saw people yelling. One little old lady in the front row, outfitted with a gray wool cardigan and matching gray bun resting above her little Grant Wood-wrinkled face, had taken her folding chair and was threatening The Viking. She hit him with the chair, and as he fell down, Ed saw him take something out of his high-top wrestling boot. The Viking was facing away from the audience and cameras, but Ed could see him clearly through the window. He pulled out a razor blade, slid it across his forehead, and then slipped it underneath the ring. When he got up, there was blood all over his face and the audience was a mixture of shouting grimaces and deer-in-the-headlights bewilderment. A trick! It was a trick! It was a show! It wasn't real! That shocked Ed. He knew that it was base and barbaric, but he'd never guessed that it wasn't real.

They moved across the hall to where KWWI's radio station broadcast the hits of the day on the *Silver Dollar Survey Show* hosted by Stan Stein, the hip DJ who was at that very moment promoting a new single by a local recording artist - *Why Oh Why'd I Make an Angel Cry* by Denny Deike (former lead singer for the Chantsmen) on the Corntones label. There stood Stan, a slender fellow in a sharkskin suit with a skinny pink tie, white shirt with black onyx cuff links, wearing a genuine smile across a quiet manner, under Everly Brothers hair. Everybody in the class shook his hand, and Stan seemed genuinely glad to be with them. He gave everyone a 45 of *Why Oh Why'd I Make an Angel Cry* - a medium-tempo early-60s formula piece with mediocre lyrics and Denny's heavily mid-ranged voice of indistinction. Quality notwithstanding, it was cool to get a fresh record from a celebrity

DJ who was a real person.

With the soybean report in the background, Ed now wondered, whatever happened to all of these people? Did Stan move to a bigger city? Did Denny ever get a better record deal? Did it matter? Why had all those guys done the things they had done? Did it make the world a better place? What had it all been for? Money? Status? That we might rock?

Ed knew it was time for some release, so he rambled out of bed ready for exercise. He went out the front door and down the steps by the big rocks that flanked the driveway, the same rocks he used to look under for worms and bugs when he was finally strong enough to lift them. He jogged by the homes of people he'd known his whole life, but hadn't thought about in years. He passed the homes of Betty Bitcher and Lucille Bitter - the town gossips, both of whom lived on Famine St. At the curve on the hill he ran by Dollardale Drive where the State Bank accountant E. Gordon Fee made his home, and where he saw Wedlock's first female Superintendent of Waterworks, Dee Hydrate, out draining her fishpond. He ran by his old babysitter Molly Mannelly's house. Frederick always thought her name sounded like a bubble bursting. He passed the home of the old pharmacist, Maude Imperative, a woman who wore white every day of her life, an aesthetic sharply contrasted by her Elvis-black hair, Joseph Stalin-moustache eyebrows, and raving purple lipstick. Crossing Main Street, he passed Wolfe Pizza with their slogan still intact - *A Howl of a Good Pizza!* - which was right next to the old refrigeration plant that still had delivery trucks with *I Only Have Ice For You* painted on their sides. Just a block further were the offices of *The Wedlock Patriarch*, a local newspaper that had been run by U. C.

Writing, who'd also owned a stationers shop named Pencilvania.

He stopped at the red light and noticed C&L Radio where he and Steve Corison used to stop after school to listen to new 45s. One time they selected a song because of its silly title, *Eight Miles High*, but wound up loving it, the Byrds, and all things 12-string electric guitar. That musical memory reminded Ed of Jamal Waters. Jamal and his family had moved from Chicago, and they were the only non-white family in the whole of Wedlock. They'd only stayed a few years, wondering at times if perhaps news of the Emancipation Proclamation of 1863 had not been delivered to Wedlock. Jamal was into music and he had turned Ed onto Big Bill Broonzy, Elmore James, and T-Bone Walker. Ed loved the passion, the rhythmic integrity, the authenticity. These guys weren't playing on top of the notes, they were going for DEEP, and they got there. Jamal used to bring records to Ed's house where they'd go to Phil's room, and, unbeknownst to Phil, borrow his green Rheems Califone record player - an older model Frederick had scored from the University when they upgraded, and which boasted a tone arm that weighed in at just under six pounds. Listening to all of those marvelous recordings had been epiphanic. To Ed it was like Dorothy opening the door to Oz, without Margaret Hamilton.

The light changed and Ed crossed the street, passing Fineldts Five-and-Dime where he'd gotten his Tiger Joe remote-control tank, and a turtle that he'd unintentionally but immediately washed down the drain while trying to prepare its new home. He ran by the house of his 4th-grade teacher Prudence Spink, a woman who used to stuff tissues in the short sleeves of her dresses that were always made from material that resembled the upholstery in her brown, be-finned Studebaker. Notwithstanding how ancillary these characters and places had seemed at the time, Ed now had a strong sense that they had been foundational in his early process.

He crossed the old railroad bridge and turned up Cedar Ridge, which took him to The Lane - the road that bordered the river that ran through Wedlock. The reeds were tapping in the breeze, the sky was all peaceful ripples of blue, silver-shadow grays and falling angles of pink - luminating layers brushing above, highlighted by sweeping sprays of lion's mane flame gold - all calming and soft, efflorescing wonder and creating a spectrum of silent strength. It was lovely.

The old Junior High was at the end of The Lane, and he saw there the visage of a boy in a red hat worn in the style of the lead character in *Then Came Bronson*, standing with one leg on the ground and one leg behind him against the building, watching other boys get sweaty playing basketball before school, and listening to the mocking and near-fights of people who seemed too coarse to entice engagement. He saw that same boy in his first band concert in that same Junior High building in the big auditorium with gilded ionic columns and a burgundy velvet stage curtain, fumbling at the beginning of *Snappy Snares* because the preceding number had been *Hiawatha*, which was a snares-disengaged selection.

As he ran, it seemed that no matter where he looked, a memory was waiting for him to notice it. He saw the maple tree where he had done his first-love carving - he'd skipped school one spring morning because he had such a crush on Corrie Parks he felt he needed to go carve her name into a tree.

He looked out upon the Tonto River and recalled the images of his first ski show, his first time in a canoe, his skating adventures over veneers of ice that left the fish on display, and the winter treks across the island that was only accessible during the frozen months. Memories just kept pouring out of the place, the details and spirit clear and alive, as though they'd occurred but two weeks earlier. It was astonishing.

Ed approached Heron Landing - a little park at the end of The Lane whose history reached out and straitjacketed him. Heron Landing was where he and Saara Liina had taken a walk on their first date. Their attraction had been instant, symbiotic, and unanimously filled with exuberance. They first noticed one another in a poetry class at the University. Then, one day, so taken by Saara's Saara-ness, he was moved by the beauty of her face to the point where the poetic spilled from his soul - he copied it down and passed it to her:

Your Face - The Soliloquy
Your Face - Exquisite -
A Miraculous Marriage of Bold & Gentle -
Such Lovely Sculpting Amidst a
    Velvet Texture of Numinous Pure
    Framed by Silken Faery-Tale Hair
    The Colour of Autumnal Moonlight,
Deep Evidencing God -
A Drama of Joy
Your Face

She smiled, embarrassed but gladdened, and their relationship was begun.

Saara was from Sweden, and a beauty highlighted by all of the

Swedish clichés - blonde, round, eloquent other-worldly features - the kind of woman whose visual glory would remain in your mind's eye for a century after only one glimpse. When Ed was with her he felt like he was touching heaven, which he was actually. On that first date he and Saara never stopped talking, except of course when they were kissing. Their coupling was Prayer. Yes, the only thing more exquisite than a beautiful woman is a beautiful woman whom one loves (and is, perhaps, unclothed). Ed slowed to a halt when he came to the spot where he and Saara had looked out upon the moon-drenched waters and talked about Shel Silversteen's *The Giving Tree*, Antoine St. Exupery's *The Little Prince*, and the Beatles. The fragrance of the occasion was animated by her un-made-up eyes that appeared as fresh flowers in a field of love. That moment had been luminous for Ed - one of those times when life seemed so wildly great that all things unreal suddenly lost their appeal.

Ed and Saara had been fast soul-mates for the whole of Ed's last year at the University of Wedlock. Their talks about the meaning of life were summarily "Yes!" They explored Beauty as a revelation of the Divine, Compassion as the heart of being community, the essence of art and the poetic as the openings to pathways of the Authentic and Mysterious. They fixed meals together, went for donuts and strong coffee at Lois's Donuts by the University three times a week where sugar, caffeine, and flavour all shook hands and invited laughter and goodness to the table. They had talked of living together. They had talked of marrying. They were in love. But when summer arrived, so did the time for Saara to go back home to Sweden. They had remained indecisive, and once she was gone, the distractions of youth and ambition quietly clouded their connection. What a loss. What a waste. It was truly tragic.

Ed had the notion to locate Saara, all these years later, but it was too good of an idea to act upon. Ed knew deep inside that someone as wonderful as she would never still be single. So what! Maybe an affair? No. That wouldn't be loving, and Ed did still love her. He cried a little and then began the walk back home. "Oh my," said Ed to himself. "Is this what it's going to mean to visit my parents? Memoryville? Soul Stabbing? What is all of this, and what am I going to do with it?!" That seemed to be the theme. Ed felt as though he was becoming drunk with his past. Where was it coming from? Why was it so vehement?

Christian Ed

Anheiserhood knocked when he got back to Frederick and Martha's. "Where did you go?" inquired Martha.

"Just around The Lane. It seems shorter than I remember it, smaller somehow."

"It's just the same as it's always been - no shorter and no longer," informed Martha, as though Ed wasn't aware of the fact that historically, Midwestern geography had remained relatively stable. "Why don't you and Daddy take the envelope over to the church?" sung Martha.

"The Envelope" - the way Frederick and Martha referred to their offering for Wedlock Lutheran, the church of Ed's childhood, the church of Frederick and Martha for over fifty years.

Ed's memories of Wedlock Lutheran were mixed. A few years earlier, Ed had heard Garrison Keillor talk about the "Sad Lutherans" on his NPR show, and Ed knew that Mr. Keillor had spoken from first-hand experience. Ed's experience wasn't so much the sadness of the Lutherans; no, he'd experienced the secondary expressions of sadness - anger, pettiness, repression, myopia, melancholia, cruelty, rampant control issues, and thriving fear.

Ed pondered his days at Wedlock Lutheran, and the memory-nazz shone forth like the Star in the East. He remembered when he and Phil used to go to Sunday services - they'd sing the hymns falsetto, and when the offering was received they'd begin humming the tune to *This Old Man*. When the plate got to their row they'd sing the chorus with the words

Nik-naks, Cadillacs,

Throw the dogs a bone.

Here's two bucks,

Now leave me alone.

It was Ed and Phil's perspective on the sincerity of some of their church family's giving. They'd heard too many comments at the annual congregational meetings - comments that affirmed the essence of their chorus.

"Sure mom. Is dad ready?"

"DADDY!" yelled Martha. Frederick came down and he and Ed were off.

"Hey dad, is Pastor Scheister still there?"

Frederick raised his eyebrows and said, "He sure is. Could you imagine him anywhere else?"

It was true. Ed could not imagine Pastor Scheister anywhere but at Wedlock Lutheran. Hell, he didn't even like imagining him there in the first place. Ed loathed Pastor Scheister. As sad as it was, there was just no other way to put it. He loathed him for what he'd been and for what he hadn't been. Ed felt that Pastor Scheister had a lot more in common with J. Edgar Hoover than he did with Jesus H. Christ. Pastor Scheister was interested in rules, laws, black and white, right and wrong, all things left-brain and linear; and of course, being a Mad Lutheran (Ed's twist on Garrison K.), Pastor Scheister's atmosphere was about as peaceful as a fresh flesh wound.

Ed hadn't always felt this way about Pastor Scheister. When he was younger, Ed was rather impressed with all of the trappings - the big robes and ornate chasubles, the pulpit in the sky, the stained glass, the carved wood, the vaulted ceilings, the platinum notes from the pipe organ - and it all seemed to revolve around the presence of Pastor Scheister. Ed had been simultaneously excited and nervous to shake Pastor Scheister's hand at the close of each service; he looked so big, and he'd been so loud - austerity came oozing out of every pore. When Ed would draw near, the scent of Pastor Scheister's Vitalis mingled with Old Spice would almost gag him. And the face - the face that appeared as though it had never smiled - would greet him with, "Good morning Mr. Anheiser." The eyes were dark, and not in a handsome way. None of it felt loving, but it'd sure been impressive.

Ed's disdain for Pastor Scheister began in the 7th grade during Confirmation classes. Frederick and Martha had always spoken about a loving God, and some of Frederick's colleagues in the Theology department would talk about having an authentic relationship with the Author of Life - about responding to the God in them that had designed them to love one another and which had made expression in the stories of the Christ figure by his compassion and abiding love for humanity. That was the stuff that Ed stopped and listened to; but that was not the stuff that Pastor Scheister talked about.

Of course, it hadn't helped matters any when some of Ed's classmates got to have Confirmation with Pastor Lebenslieb - a man who Ed thought might have been Jesus returned. Pastor Lebenslieb smiled easily and often - his eyes were soft and sincere, and he did much more listening than talking. Whenever he was in a room, Ed felt as though it was a safe and happy place. In retrospect, Ed understood it as the presence of God incarnate. But Pastor Lebenslieb only lasted a year at Wedlock Lutheran. Pastor Scheister was always competing, always critical of and negative about Pastor Lebenslieb, and since Pastor Scheister was the head pastor, and the church council was as hierarchical, controlling, conventional, and dysfunctional as Pastor Scheister, when Pastor Scheister recommended that everyone get a raise except Pastor Lebenslieb (and the council adopted it), Pastor Lebenslieb realized he was fighting a hopeless situation. He left in June, and Pastor Scheister never mentioned him again. Pastor Scheister got the church to call one of his old classmates, Pastor Lurch - a Scheister clone who helped keep the place void of the Divine.

The experience so frustrated Ed that during his second year of Confirmation with Pastor Lurch, Ed and his friend August Rheibold asked if they could receive extra credit by putting their favourite Bible verses on wooden plaques with a wood-burning set Augie had gotten for Christmas. Both pastors thought it was a splendid idea - it made them feel as though they were inspiring pastors, which was true. They had inspired Ed and Augie to this. Their only recommendation was that the boys limit it to one verse per plaque, that way the verses would be easier to memorize. Both Scheister and Lurch were imbibed with the notion that short-term memory brings one closer to God.

Every day after school, Ed and Augie poured over the Bible, and then took the fruits of their labour and burned them into wood - dozens of pieces of fallen trees which then held "the words of the Lord." Ed and Augie asked if they could present their efforts before both Confirmation classes, and the pastors agreed. So, on a cold late-winter evening in the Parish Hall, Ed and Augie stood before fifty-three confirmands and presented their plaques. Pastor Lurch, who'd been excited about the idea from the start, gave the introduction. "These two young men, your classmates, have been inspired to take their favourite Bible verses and burn them into history for all to read. I hope some of the rest of you will follow their fine example." He turned towards Ed and Augie with a wimpy smile and said, "Mr. Anheiser, Mr. Rheibold, proceed."

Ed and Augie stood up, went over to Ed's blue Radio Flyer loaded with the biblically-engraved plaques, and began holding them up one and at time, reading them aloud. The first was, "Slew they the goats and put their bits in pots." Next came, "And if the hair has fallen out from the front of his head, he has baldness of the forehead." Then, "Essau was a hairy man, but I am smooth." More gems of wisdom followed - "I went down into the garden of nuts." Followed by, "Thou shalt not kick the pricks." And when Ed and Augie simultaneously recited, "Thou shalt not covet thy neighbor's ass," Pastor Scheister broke in. He had been furiously looking through his Bible to check the accuracy of their scholarship, and indeed, they were right. He couldn't chastise them - there was no ground. Pastor Lurch had been sitting there looking on as though he'd just been forced to watch bestial pornography.

More than a few confirmands were bright red with unreleased laughter - tears falling, heads down, hands over mouths, sputtering bursts of choked laughter echoing through the Parish Hall. Pastor Scheister stopped them with a clearing of the throat. "Well, thank you Mr. Anheiser, Mr. Rheibold, but we really must be getting to our worksheets. Everybody back to class!" at which point Pastor Scheister walked out. Pastor Lurch was left sitting, stupefied. Ed and Augie smiled at one another and shook hands. Triumph!

Essentially it was a very sad moment. Though they couldn't have worded it so at the time, Ed and Augie had indeed shown

Scheister and Lurch what sort of fruit their "inspiration" was bearing: Meaninglessness. Accurate uselessness. Confusing truth with the facts and reducing the Bible to the concrete. If only once Pastor Scheister would have talked about the Mystery of God, the Unknowable; that the Bible and the commandments were made for us, not us for them; that the Decalogue was a gift to help us understand how life worked, not a set of rules to follow so you didn't get in trouble with the Sky Daddy. Neither of the pastors ever revealed anything about the true nature of the Divine - the Light of Love shining in the essence of our beings that we might respond with the same and love one another, seek one another's highest good, make the fruits of the spirit verbs which were illustrative of the blessing of Life. Those truths were never broached. Lurch and Scheister's methodology inspired Ed and Augie to burn "Essau was a hairy man, but I am smooth" into a piece of pine and then laugh about it. That was why Ed loathed Pastor Scheister: for all of the stupidity which he had enforced, and for all of the Divine that he had deprived him of.

Frederick and Ed pulled up by the side of the Parish Hall and walked up the marble steps. Ed turned around and surveyed the parking lot, and a scene from a Thanksgiving long ago appeared before him. During a Thanksgiving Eve service of Ed's youth, Wedlock had received the blessing of a blizzard. When everyone came out to the parking lot, it was snowing madly - lovely but treacherous. While Ed waited for Frederick to bring the car around, he heard spinning tires and yelling. Off to his left was the Babbit's brown Ford Torino rocking back and forth. Ernie and Eleanor Babbit were friends of Frederick and Martha, and Ernie was a colleague at the University, head of the Philosophy department. Ernie may have been effective as a professor of philosophy, but he didn't appear to have much of a gift for snow navigation, nor patience. He had his shoulder to the back bumper of the Torino, sweat forming under his narrow-brimmed 50's newspaperman-like Stetson. His two-toned glasses were slipping down his Martini-veined beak as his face screwed up in the "I-just-had-a-lemon" expression. Ed heard him yell, "OK!" which must have been the signal for Eleanor to floor it, and floor it she did - the result being an avalanche of tire-driven snow spraying all over Ernie, followed by the back end of the car sliding sideways like a crab, knocking him flat. There he lay, sprawled out like a murder victim, shouting "For Corn Sake Eleanor! What Was That?! Goddammit Mrs. Babbit! (Ed loved the alliteration) Get me up! Get Me UP!" It made Ed smile then, and he was smiling now. He looked down at the steps and remembered the last time he saw Pastor Scheister's sister, Adolphina Scheister, on these very steps, seething with anger and screaming as she'd just cancelled her membership at Wedlock Lutheran because the pages in the hymnal were too thin.

They went through the doors and into the church offices. There sat Pastor Scheister, reading a novel entitled *The Mysteries of Akron*, wearing his uniform - a black polyester cleric, black polyester pants, and a pair of scuffed-up wingtips (black) with polyester laces. He looked the same only older. It had always bewildered Ed that a pastor would wear those lifeless clerics - if anyone might know the exuberance of the Divine, surely it would be a spiritual guide, one whom God had called. It was as though Pastor Scheister thought the old camp song went, *And they'll know we are Christians by our shirts, by our shirts, yes they'll know we are Christians by our shirts.* Ed knocked on the door and said "Hello." Pastor Scheister startled, spilling his cup of coffee onto the video on his desk, that epic film classic - *Thyroid Disorders and You.* One would have thought he'd just been caught with the church secretary in his lap.

"Yes, can I help you?" came Pastor Scheister's reply. Of course, he didn't recognize Ed.

Frederick responded, "We're just here to drop off the envelope - here you go."

"Yes, yes, thank you," replied Pastor Scheister as he put the book into the second drawer of his metal desk. They made some uncomfortable small talk, and while Frederick and Pastor Scheister were visiting, Ed walked over to the sanctuary. It, too, was the same - some fresh paint and some new banners, but the same. And like The Lane, it looked much smaller than he'd remembered it. So much had happened here. He was baptized here. He was confirmed here. He lost his Jawbreakers over the balcony here.

He looked around at the stained glass windows - they were all the same - scenes from the Bible with writing underneath in German (which he later learned was there to inform everyone who it was that'd had enough money to get their names on the windows to accommodate their egos and their denial-of-death disorders). Ed used to look at them when Pastor Scheister was droning on about something from the pulpit. There was the scene where Jesus was talking to Mary Magdalene, both looking intent and profound, in keeping with the stories. Ed used to imagine these windows coming to life - Jesus kissing her on the neck, then slowly pulling her robe from her shoulders, revealing her miraculous breasts - Mary breathing deeply with her eyes closed and her mouth slightly open, hair cascading over her shoulders; Jesus caressing her like a man in love.

On the other side of the sanctuary there was a scene depicting men walking through the desert - backs straight, tireless, bold, the one leading them holding his right hand in the air with what appeared to be a gesture of greeting. Ed always imagined the lead figure turning his hand sideways and saying, "Geez, it's hot out here. That sun is driving me nuts! Anybody got a hat?" Up in the balcony there was a smaller window that depicted Jesus with his head slightly cocked, knocking on a door. Ed imagined him saying, "Hello? Hello? I'm from St. Ralph's - here for the annual Stewardship Drive."

Ed walked to the center of the chancel where they used to place a cornucopia every Thanksgiving - a huge rattan Horn o' Plenty that had fruits and vegetables flowing from its center - a grand symbol of bounty indeed. He also remembered when they tried some newer-styled worship services - it was the first time Ed had ever seen drums in church. There in the middle of the chancel was a drum kit that looked like Ringo's, being played with vigour by a student from the University. When the service was over, Ed remembered Martha's huffy response - "Well! All that was missing was the beer and pretzels." She and Frederick used to refer to it as 'The Ya Ha Service'. It was not a compliment, and their perspective was not lost on Ed. How was it that they acknowledged a God who was revealed as one who kept trying to set people free, while they embraced the bondage theology of *the way we've always done it*? Had they forgotten that Martin Luther was labeled "heretic" for having new understandings? Guess so.

Then Ed recalled the time his mom's brother, Uncle Herald, had served as assisting minister. Pastor Scheister had heard that Martha's brother was an ordained Lutheran pastor and Christian author, so he invited him to participate in a service when he heard that Uncle Herald would be visiting during the winter. What Pastor Scheister didn't know was that Uncle Herald's perspectives and writings were a combination of mystic theology and humour - things that Pastor Scheister would have known nothing about, and therefore would have labeled "the work of the devil." And he'd never seen Uncle Herald's bumper sticker - *Pastors Do It With Spirit.*

On a third Sunday in Advent, Uncle Herald began the service at Wedlock Lutheran with, "Why don't we all open our hymnals and sing that old classic Lutheran hymn, *I Want a Red Hot Mamma and An Ice-Cold Beer.*" All of the ushers turned red. Pastor Scheister froze. Ed covered his mouth with both hands to impede an instantaneous laugh that erupted from his core, one that would have filled the sanctuary. Martha put her hand to her face in a block-the-light gesture as she lowered her head and whispered, "Oh Herald." Mrs. Purselipps, the organist, launched into *The Old Rugged Cross* while Uncle Herald smiled to himself. After that, the service went along as usual until Uncle Herald got up to read the second lesson. "Today's lesson is from the first letter of Paul to the Ephesians. I'll be translating from the original Greek that we might get an even deeper understanding into the mind of Paul." He began, "I Paul, an apostle of the Gospel of Christ, believe ... that Martians are stealing my luggage." One older lady in the front pew choked out her cherry Sucret, launching it skyward into Mrs. Schoenstedt's blue fresh-from-Ramona's-House-of-Beauty hair. Mrs. Purselipps passed out and fell forward onto the organ console, producing an eruption of sound that made everyone sense that perhaps Wedlock was experiencing its first earthquake. Pastor Scheister jumped up immediately and began clearing his throat and thumbing through the Bible to get right on to the Gospel text. Ed was grinning from ear to ear. It was one of his best memories from his time at Wedlock Lutheran.

"Look familiar?" queried Frederick from the narthex.

"Yep, very," replied Ed. Frederick smiled and joined him by the baptismal font.

"Do you remember when we baptized Gigi?" asked Frederick. Gigi was Ed's little sister who was now living in Berlin as an artist of budding note with a day gig that had her working with special-needs children. Ed always felt as though Gigi was the one who'd "made it out." She was seemingly undaunted by her history, whereas Ed felt as though phantoms of Wedlock visited him like Dickens' Ghost of Christmas Past, without the happy ending. Ed remembered the baptism, and felt his loneliness for Gigi.

"Didn't Phil and I stand next to you and Mr. and Mrs. Dobelis?"

"That's right," smiled Frederick, as he looked through the altar.

"How's Gigi? How's Meta (Dobelis)?"

Frederick responded, "Gigi's fine - she's having a showing this autumn at some gallery there in Berlin; and she's invented some device to help the physically challenged kids she works with hold mallets when they play Orff instruments."

Ed smiled, twinkled his eyes, and nodded. Frederick paused before adding, "Didn't your mother tell you about Meta? She said she was going to tell you."

"Tell me what?"

"She was diagnosed with bone cancer and spent the last six months in and out of the hospital for treatments. She died last week and we went to her funeral the day before you came home."

No, Martha hadn't told Ed, and the news shocked him, a lot. He had known Meta well - in some ways she'd been a bit of a second mom. He'd mowed her yard, raked her leaves, and put up her Christmas tree every year he'd lived in Wedlock after Deutsch (her husband) had died. Frederick continued, "She fought it hard and kept up a good disposition right up to the end. She always had a good disposition," he said, almost to himself.

Ed was quiet. She'd more than a good disposition. Meta Dobelis was one of the few people Ed had ever met who he felt had lived a deeply meaningful life, though she'd every reason not to. She and Deutsch had arrived in America after fleeing Lithuania during Hitler's rise to power. The Lutheran Church had helped people relocate during that dark period in Western history, and the Dobelises had been assigned to Wedlock. They arrived shaken and bewildered, as would anyone. Not only had they left their country and all that they had known and had, they also left their son who'd been sick with the measles when they were scheduled to depart. Plans had been made for him to come over following his recovery, but by the time he knew health, the borders were closed. They never heard from him again.

Not long after they'd arrived, Deutsch began working as a janitor for Wedlock Lutheran, even though he'd been a professor of European Music History at a Lithuanian university. When he was asked to speak about his life in Europe at a Lion's Club meeting, nobody believed him when he told them of the atrocities occurring there. After that he was guarded about his friendships, and Ed always felt as though Deutsch had never really moved to America - he often had a sad and distant look in his eyes. He loved to sit on the front porch of their modest home and listen to the international news as the day prepared for bed.

Frederick and Martha befriended the Dobelises and treated them as family, which was Ed's entree into their lives. Ed recalled their home - the kitchen table of Formica and chrome where Meta would serve him homemade lemonade and bacon rolls - a Meta specialty - after his lawn work; the old tweed couch and the iron-frame beds that had been donated by the Augsburg-Trinity-Matins-Luther-Bach-Oktoberfest-Sauerkraut-und-Brats Women's Circle of Wedlock Lutheran. There wasn't a piece of furniture or decoration in the place that had any monetary value, but Ed loved the atmosphere. It was humble. It was real. There weren't even any light switches - all of the overhead lighting was activated by pull-chains. Ed thought it gave the house character.

One time, after a furious session of leaf raking, Ed and Meta were talking about material things - Ed was already looking forward to his Christmas gifts just nine weeks away. He asked Meta, "Is there any 'thing' in your life that you've always wanted?" She looked off towards the toaster on the scarred red linoleum counter, turned back to him and replied, "You know, I've always wanted a clothes dryer. I don't mind hanging out the wash in the summer, but I've never liked hanging it around the basement during the cold months. Yes, a clothes dryer would have been nice. But that's about it."

Ed was speechless. A clothes dryer? Didn't everyone have a clothes dryer? How much could that cost - a few hundred dollars? Her one wish in the material realm was a clothes dryer? Not a castle? Full-length mink coat? Bentley limo? A clothes dryer? Really? Ed thought about that off and on for years, and the memory now made him shake his head with a deep smile. What a profound woman. Surely, God sang with verve in the life and soul of Meta Dobelis.

"Why didn't you tell me?" asked Ed, sounding a little angry.

Frederick got defensive in his usual way, "Your mother said she was going to tell you! It's not my fault!"

The church moment was broken and they walked out to the car without any more discussion. There wasn't anything to say. Ed was very sad about Meta being gone, and he felt bad about having missed her funeral. Frederick felt bad that Ed felt bad.

First Hudson, now Meta - people in Ed's life who had mattered, were formative, and were now gone. It stopped Ed. In his mind, Wedlock was changeless, static, a frozen piece of history. But it wasn't. For the first time ever, Ed realized that even things Wedlock change. He looked over at Frederick driving the car with his old sunglasses on. Ed could see the fan of deepened lines by the sides of Frederick's eyes, and his posture was not what it had once been - he seemed to be shrinking. He sensed his dad's deteriorations and pondered the ever-nearing visit of mortality.

He kept staring at Frederick and recalled the time Frederick had taken him to his first day of kindergarten at the Kindergarten House, a one-story light-blue farmhouse from the turn of the century across the street from the Parish Hall of Wedlock Lutheran. Frederick drove the family's new (but used) bronze Impala on a brisk-and-sunny autumn day - Frederick with his dark wavy hair, camel-coloured car coat, fresh skin and an air of excitement-cum-anxiety about his youngest (pre-Gigi) entering school. Ed cried and cried while Frederick calmly told him he'd be back before lunch to pick him up. Before the morning was over, Ed was marching around the room with his forefingers in his ears singing *Onward Christian Soldiers* - a behaviour that earned Ed a stern look and loud voice from Miss Kurt - a fifty-ish maiden who had devoted her life to kindergarten Lutherans. When Frederick came to gather him from school, Ed was a little teary, and Frederick embraced him with the softness and strength of the love of God. They didn't exchange many words - there was no need. The hug said it all.

As he looked over at Frederick in his aging state, Ed realized that his childhood memories were all over - there would be no more. It was a stark revelation and it came without warning. There was Frederick, an old, stable-but-fragile man who probably didn't have many years left, finite to the earth. The days of going downtown on a Friday night (the one evening when the stores were open) and "prowling around," as Frederick liked to call it, looking for Hot Wheels (an early obsession for Ed) were over. The Saturday afternoons of mowing the yard with the new red power mower from Niewohner's Hardware, and then playing catch, were over. The visits to the library so that father and son could check out books that took them to other places, were over. It was all in the past. Ed's realization made him feel as though his history in Wedlock had just been sealed. The story was, perhaps, over.

Adult Ed

They arrived back at 101 Home Blvd. and got out of the car in silence. Ed said, "I think I'm gonna take a walk. Wanna come with me?"

"No thanks. I'm going to see what your mother is up to. We eat at six."

Ed nodded and walked down the hill towards the old graffiti-covered water tower - *Class of '87 ... Julie Rocks!* His eyes were fixed on the pavement and his heart was fixed on the present.

He walked and walked. He was confused and unsettled. Thoughts raced through his head - thoughts that didn't make any sense, or maybe they made too much sense. He groped for clarity. Wedlock. His discomfort with his place in life. His own self-esteem issues beaten into unraveled by the unspoken crazy German motto "Mess up and you deserve to die." It had taught him to be driven, but he wanted to be driving. It felt like he was in a society that had ignored its soul for the longest time. Was he in the wrong culture? That's what he'd thought when he left Wedlock and moved to Chicago, but in some ways things weren't really that much different in the big city. Sure, it had its own hipness, but it also had a coldness, and in some ways it was worse. He felt separate from people there too. He felt disconnected from nature. He felt that his intimacy with humanity was deeply abrogated. He wondered if maybe he'd just pulled a geographic - thinking that externals would fix his internals. Despite some "success" in his work and even some national notoriety, it didn't feel real - it felt evanescent, pseudo-life, just accolades from a bunch of contrived systems of socialized conventions that offered no real nourishment.

He thought about his college friend, Stephen Splendour - an intelligent and sometimes kind fellow who had covered himself with worldly success. They had met in a literature class at the University of Wedlock: Literature 301B, taught by Professor Thurmann Belleville. They spent the entire semester on *Moby Dick* because Professor Belleville had done his doctoral thesis on "The Linguistic Motifs of 19th Century Aquatic Language and How They Relate to Our Current Understandings of Blubber and Corsets." A better name for the class would have been "A Downpour of Stone-Faced Mind-Numbing Sharkshit." After the first week, Ed and Stephen would get stoned on hashish right before class and pass notes:

"Isn't it fun studying Moby DICK?"

"I'd rather study DICKens."

"Really? I prefer Emily DICKinson."

"She's good, but I like DICK Tracy."

"I've got a good idea for a novel - it's a sci-fi about the re-fi of a hi-fi by Eli the French guy from Shanghai who flies the red eye to Lodi singing *Jambalaya* and *My Guy* sipping Nehi Chai Mai-Tais."

"Cool! What's the title?

"The Case of The Barking Pumpkin."

They'd throw wild parties where at four in the morning everyone would wind up dancing to Stax records while old silent films were projected onto the ceiling, and out in the yard people would be dressed in sheets trying to depict faeries, enacting improvised scenes from *A Midsummer Night's Dream*. One time they almost wound up in jail. During one of the parties they went in someone's van to get chips, dip, and some organic shade-grown fair-trade bubble gum. The driver of the van took off before Ed and Stephen could close the sliding side doors, so they just left them open. When the police pulled them over, they looked in the back where Ed and Stephen were sitting. As they waved their flashlights around, one of the officers said, "You guys got any open beers in there?" Stephen held up a full, open can of Grain Belt and said, "Just some empties." Ed tried to use visual imagery to make the opium in his front pocket disappear. The other officer spoke to his partner. "Doncha think we oughtta have a look around inside the van?" The first officer said, "Naw. You guys just close the door and take it easy. Nice van." And they left.

After college, Ed had gone on to graduate school while Stephen began working with his dad's international consulting business, which, essentially, told people what they wanted to hear and oppressed third world countries for a thousand dollars an hour. Despite their different lives they'd stayed in touch, as Stephen had an office in Chicago. Then one day, Ed got a call. After months of commuting between New York, Chicago, and Los Angeles, Stephen had felt cascadingly poorly - for the better part of a week he'd been declining, so he called Ed to take him to the Emergency Room. There on the table lay Stephen in his custom-tailored suit, special edition Rolex, exercised body and beautifully coiffed hair, pleading with the doctor, "Please help me ... Please!" Within the hour he was dead. Burnout. The successful worldling with all of the trappings of economic grandeur and luxury lay lifeless on a stainless-steel table under humming fluorescent lights, his trophy wife crying in confusion over the American

Dream revealed in the fruit of its insanity. He'd spent his life on his ego and his livelihood. Ed had watched it. He'd envied Stephen. Part of him liked to be condescending by thinking that Stephen had "sold out," which was true, but another part of him wished that he'd been Stephen. There lay part of Ed's dream - dead on the table. Ed had shuddered - at his friend's death, and at the illusion laid bare right before his eyes. Luxury and an illusory worldview had come as guests to take a slave, even unto death. Oh, the ways we are held by the villainage of our own inviting.

He turned the corner by the old movie theater, the Elite, and walked towards the abandoned railroad bridge. Then, loud and clear, seemingly out of nowhere, he heard one of his own Ed-isms:

How You Live is What You Believe

What You Fill Your Life Up With is What It Becomes Full Of

He'd felt so good about those insights when they'd been given to him in moments of Revelation. But now, instead of being abstract truisms, he had to face how those truths intersected with his own living. Tall order.

Ed found his way to the old train depot that had been converted into a coffee shop - Java Junction. He sat down with a beautifully rendered Americano and watched the steam from the cup rise and curl in the gloaming sunlight - it looked like Da Vinci's drawings of water in motion, resurrected to help him clarify his reflections. Ed pondered how he'd been living. Was his living confluent with his beliefs? Maybe that was the angst, the rub, the bee in all this jam. Ed wondered whether or not his anxiety might not be a cue for growth - real growth. What if he framed it that way? For as long as he could recall he'd been hypersensitive to criticism, negativity, and the injustices of the world. Maybe it was genetic - after all, Grandma Bumgartner was the type who'd get a new hat and then refuse to wear it in public because she just knew that people would think, "Well! Who does she think she is?" Which, in Wedlock, was probably true. But the real question was Grandma B's own - "Who am I and what does that mean?" Maybe that was Ed's question - the existential biggie. His responses to life's cruelties, absurdities, and disappointments had been sarcasm, cynicism, and condescension taken to fever pitch - responses that gave him a false and fleeting sense of superiority - responses that gained the approval of his friends and were cause for much laughter, but for what? To focus on what life wasn't? Protection to blunt the hurt of affront - make fun of something before it makes fun of you, and affirms your own deep voices that whisper what you're not, in an eloquent endless oration in the spirit of hell?

How You Live is What You Believe

What You Fill Your Life Up With is What It Becomes Full Of

Ed had a sense that the abyss between his truths and his behaviours was cavernous. He'd been letting his perceptions of everyone and everything Wedlock define too many parts of his living. Much of his life had been comprised of unhealthy responses to sick behaviours and psyches, and it simply wasn't working to let the angers, discontentments, unawarenesses, and confusions of others spill onto him and stain his spirit. Why had he let that happen?

He took a sip of his coffee and looked at the Regulator clock pendulum swinging back and forth, and as he began to critique the aesthetics of the clock, he wondered if, perhaps, his judgments about others signaled his judgments about himself. He recalled one of the back-room conversations he'd had with Frederick when they discussed that revelation of the Divine that came in the form of the invitation that we might love one another as we love ourselves. Ed now felt the nod of reality when he sensed that that's about what he had done. Ed hadn't been compassionate towards others because he hadn't been capable of compassion towards himself. He'd heard so much about what he wasn't from the voices of the people who had heard the same thing their whole lives, that it was but a skip and a jump to look back at all of the ways he'd dipped his ego biscuits into the beverage of life and tasted their bitter yet alluring-by-familiarity essence right out of the cup of fear.

All of this hit Ed like a stigmata - so pure and holy that it made clear a lifetime of practiced behaviours that blocked life in the present. YEOW! This dose of naked reality startled him with such a power because it was so personal.

For as long as he could remember he had deflected compliments because they didn't compute. He'd learned it as a boy watching Frederick recite poetry at the annual Writer's Workshop at the University - Frederick would offer a truly moving rendition of Chaucer, and as people would greet him with authentic encomiums, Frederick would look at his shoes, shake his head from side to side, up and down, and rub his fingers against his palms in mute confusion. It was sad.

Then Ed remembered his encounter with a student from South Africa named Gottlieb Gronlund. He had met Gottlieb the summer before he entered the University of Wedlock. Uncle Herald had come to know some students from South Africa when he taught a class in Liberation Theology at Cape Town University, and

Gottlieb wound up coming to America to do an independent study in the theology of Mott the Hoople at the University of Wedlock with one of Uncle Herald's colleagues from his Berkeley days, Professor Psilocybin, who was funded by a fellowship from M&Ms. Professor Psilocybin had had a career as a songwriter for a fundamentalist rock band called Guns'n'Moses, but soon switched to myth and fiction when the nonfiction of fundamentalism became too frightening.

Gottlieb was a genteel and sedate fellow who had seen tragedies unimaginable during apartheid. Ed learned that Reverend Gronlund's real name had been Bumbashooti, but the missionaries made him change it, and mandated suit and tie for all occasions. Ed remembered getting frustrated: "Why would you trade a colourful name for some archaic German relic, and a cool dashiki for the uniform of the oppressor?" He had judged Gottlieb for his choices - things that Ed had felt were concessions to warped Western ways. Ed now recalled that encounter as a blaring example of what he'd become so good at in adulthood - the same behaviour that stilts one's soul to sourdom. He shut his eyes in a squinty way and whispered to himself, "Why did it matter to me what this sensitive African fellow did, wore, or called himself? Why did I have to go and generalize my perspectives to him? I hadn't the slightest idea of what he'd been through! Why would I expect him to think like me? Why did I have to go and judge him? That's the behavior that I loathe so much about my patterning! Damn! Why couldn't I have just asked him what it was like to be a spiritual guide to people in rural Africa and listened with openness to his thoughtful response? That would have been enlightening! But NO, I had to start pretending that he was *me*, so I could rail at the ways of the world that bother *me*! Maybe Bumbashooti had been hornswoggled, but that was his business, not mine. Why did I do that? Eminent stark narcissism expressed as dumb!"

It wasn't dumbness, actually, it was just how *Ed* had been exampled. His behaviour with Bumbashooti wasn't much different than that of the missionaries who had encouraged European names and suit-and-tie for rural African travel - it was simply the fruit of judgment, control, and arrogance - the offspring of frightendom that so often consumes life, or rather, supplants it. Some call it a human trait for its prevalence in recorded history, but Ed thought that it wasn't a trait - not really. It was a behaviour - a behaviour that could have been altered much sooner for Ed if he'd been a better host to Awareness. *How I live is what I believe. What I fill my life up with is what it becomes full of.* The truth is always simple, it's just not easy. *And the Truth will set me free, but only if I claim the freedom.* He recalled learning the etymology of the word "sarcasm": *a tearing of the flesh.* That's about what it felt like. He'd been tearing his life with his confused foci.

Ed reached back for moments of joy and that which had been life giving. He remembered the time Frederick had taken him over to Buel's Bicycles to get his first bike. Old Mr. Buel lived in the only home in Wedlock that was in the ground - all that gave any indication that it was a dwelling at all was a doorway that poked its way out from the lot, a tired green mailbox mounted on a set of handlebars, and a homemade sign that read *Buel's Bicycles* staked in the front yard. Actually, the place was an old bomb-shelter that Mr. Buel converted into a home/bike shop not long after he'd gotten back from serving in the Korean War. Mr. Buel wore an immense smile upon a face that was as smooth and happy as an apple. He had slick black hair about half-an-inch long that looked like a lawn of fresh-mown licorice, and cheap but neat clothing.

Father and son had descended the stairway that seemed as though it sloped at about a 45-degree angle, and at the bottom of the steps off to the right were eleven used bicycles as clean as a hospital, and to the left stood three new designs with banana seats and high-rise handlebars. They selected one of the new ones - a metallic gold Stingray with a leopard-skin seat, and red-and-yellow flames billowing from the chain guard that had been handpainted by Mr. Buel with the exactness of the High Renaissance. The bike was wheeled up the steps and into the trunk of the bronze Impala. On the ride home, Ed recalled Frederick and Martha's arguments about money he'd overheard earlier in the springtime - both of them frustrated that there wasn't enough of it to take the annual trip to the Dakotas and pay for the kids' swimming lessons and bikes. He turned to look at Frederick and sighed with gratitude - Ed knew that Frederick had worked construction digging out basements during the summer so that he could have a moment like the one he was enjoying.

His summer memories came forward to sparkle in their beauty - candy-sweet corn alongside cucumbers and onions in sour cream, and fresh peaches that came from a never-ending parade of peach crates that Martha stored under the basement stairs to keep them cool. Swimming in the Wedlock Municipal Pool with an array of true friends and lovely visages of beautifully developed girls in bikinis. A&W root beer in those paper-sealed-with-wax containers that looked like old megaphones. Balmy evenings at the Youth Center, watching girls move and bands play. It was the first time he'd ever experienced rock music in three dimensions - guys with tight clothing, long hair, and the skill of the best riffing through Marshall amplifier stacks at volume levels that shook Ed's bell-bottoms. Ed recalled the band Able Mable and their guitar player, Ned Zeplin, whom everyone called 'Orange' because he always wore an orange scarf when he gigged. Ed could still see him as plain as day, there on the stage of the Youth Center amidst dim colourful lights, with expression pouring out of his presence in the ways of spontaneous vibrant art that shook the corrugated building down to the concrete slab and left Ed gaping in awe at one of the wonders of humanity - new music that danced with the integrity of the ages.

He remembered the time Frederick and Martha took him to see Buddy Rich at Mister Kelly's nightclub in Chicago. Ed had become enamoured with Buddy after he'd seen him on *The Tonight Show* with Johnny Carson. To Ed, Buddy Rich was a savant both as a musician and as a wit. Ed would get special dispensation from Frederick and Martha to stay up late whenever Buddy was to appear on TV, and then he'd tape record it with Phil's new portable tape recorder. He still had some of the old cassettes. Ed was smitten, and when he learned from a *Downbeat* magazine that Buddy was going to be in Chicago, he asked Frederick and Martha if they'd take him, and without hesitation they said they would.

They drove seven hours in the heat of the summer for that event, and Ed sat about ten feet away from Buddy - right in the front, just to the left of Buddy's ride cymbal. Frederick and Martha had dinner, but Ed was too stunned to do anything but study Buddy. He was wearing a white Nehru jacket with an Aztecpatterned medallion, short dry-ish hair (was it a toupee?), and that concentrated hound-dog-face expression hovering over brilliant brass cymbals and white pearled drums all held up by silver singing stands. What music! Genius technique employed only for the purpose of genius art. The drum rolls sounded like someone was pouring finely granulated sugar, and the solo with brushes was like the voice of the heavens depicted in the ceiling of the Sistine Chapel. And Ed was there! Now he really knew what Mr. Messerschmidt's relationship with Shot Jackson had been like. After the music, Frederick got Buddy's autograph for Ed, and as Frederick was explaining to Buddy that it was for his thirteen-year-old son, Buddy smiled, walked over to where Ed was sitting, and gave Ed his brushes. Ed still had them.

While they were there on their drum-inspired trip to Chicagoland, they also got to tour the Ludwig Drum factory on Damen Avenue. Frederick's great grandfather had been William F. Ludwig Sr.'s pastor, so Frederick's parents had known the man responsible for most of the advances in 20th century American percussion history. Ed had seen Ludwig drums on *The Ed Sullivan Show* when the Beatles hit American television in February of 1964, so the name Ludwig had unparalleled credibility with Ed.

On the tour of the plant they saw the red-carpeted boardroom with an oval rosewood table that looked like it could accommodate at least ninety people, bordered by glass cases lined in purple velvet, housing engraved brass snare drums that elicited scenes of the Jazz Age. Just looking at the drums, Ed could almost hear the wet cracking backbeat amidst a sea of dancing art deco Chicagoans in satin waistcoats and silk taffeta gowns laughing with the exuberance of the mystery of that love affair between music, movement, and pure joy. The Ludwig patriarch himself had guided the tour. The place was an odd mixture of gleaming new drums and the growl of groaning gears, with men and women of all races, creeds, and colours doing psyche-numbing work in the heat of Chicago summer. Mr. Ludwig was gracious, kind, and smiling, except when they got to that portion of the factory where the drumsticks were being made - where he, Ed, and the rest of the family noticed a foldout of a glorious gently grinning expression of unclothed femininity tacked upon one of the machines. The gray flannel-suited CEO turned red, scowled, and ripped the adorable two-dimensional siren from her place on the lathe, tossing her miraculous visage into the nearest waste can. Ed was a bit scared at the volatility, and a bit sad to see something so primally beautiful discarded.

The family had always made an annual trek to the Chicago Art Institute to stay connected with that part of the culture that didn't exist much in Wedlock. In his memory, the trip had always been laborious. When the bronze Impala died, Frederick got a blue VW Beetle, and five people in an old Bug is its own artwork. It wasn't as though the Art Institute held a lot of enthusiasm for Ed before he hit puberty. Highlights of the trip included the prolonged hope that Frederick would stop at a hamburger stand in Savanna called *The Hamburger Stand* (Frederick was to explain to Ed that to many people in rural Illinois, a pragmatic descriptive was indistinguishable from poetry). Their hamburgers boasted a sauce like Thousand Island dressing that tasted as though it had actually come from the Thousand Islands - a concoction that blended sweet and sour and texture in a way that had the taste buds cheering at the mere sight of the signage for The Hamburger Stand. The first time they'd stopped at the place it was out of bathroom desperation. Frederick was the sort of traveler who liked to "get there," perhaps even at the expense of ruptured bladders all around. Once they'd used the relief-room, Frederick felt so comfortable that some comfort food felt like the natural thing to do. On every subsequent trip, the family would blend passive-aggressive - "Isn't it almost lunchtime dad? You know, I heard french fries were real good this year in Illinois - we read about it in our *Weekly Reader*" with the all-out there-are-no-options battle cry of, "If we don't stop, I'm gonna jump!" Frederick would tease sometimes, pretend not to hear, turn at the last minute, drive by and then laugh when anarchy and rebellion turned into verbs. But, they always stopped. Sometimes they'd stop in Galena, that time-honored hamlet that always smelled of boxwood, at an old Victorian house that had been turned into a restaurant named Victorian House Restaurant (more rural Illinois poetry). Ed recalled feeling uncomfortable being waited upon by an old black man in a white tuxedo - it felt stereotypically cruel by its historical reference.

Ed's earliest recollection at the Art Institute was plopping himself down upon a circular couch in the middle of the Impressionists room, sliding around the creme-coloured vinyl donut taking in brilliant art at the rate of three seconds per masterpiece, pronouncing himself finished, "I'm Done", in under a minute, and then sighing as he slumped down into the "I'm Bored" position. They went for lunch al fresco right there at the museum amidst broad umbrellas that guarded wrought-iron tables and chairs which had sturdy and artful written all over their

demeanors. Ed was shocked the first time he viewed the menu -
the entrees and their prices seemed otherworldly to him at the
time:

Roast Peacock Tongue - Thirty-seven Dollars

Cream of Daddy-Long-Legs Soup - Eighteen Dollars

Braised Duck Feces - Twenty-six Dollars

Ed looked at Frederick and Martha with wide, blinking eyes
and asked, "Can I get whatever I want?" swallowing with difficulty
at the thought of Cream of Daddy-Long-Legs Soup.

"What do you want?" came the parental chorus.

"How 'bout a hamburger, french fries, and a Coke?"

"That's fine, but I don't think they've got french fries today - it
looks like it's potato salad," said Frederick.

"OK," was Ed's quick response.

After his food arrived, Ed felt safe, but upon eyeing the potato
salad, he noticed that someone had put pepper on it, "Hey, what's
the deal?" frowned Ed.

"What?"

"Who put pepper on my potato salad?" said Ed, as he pointed
to the mayo-coloured scoop.

Frederick and Martha looked at one another with sad,
knowing smiles as Frederick shook his slightly bowed head three
times. Very softly he said, "That's not pepper Ed, it's pollution.
We're downtown, you know. Just wipe it off and eat it quickly,"
which is what Ed did.

He also marveled at the bewildering conversations around
him. At the very next table sat a fellow in a lovely light-aqua linen
suit speaking in a patter Ed would later learn to associate with
Woody Allen - "I, I, I don't understand why she gets so upset? I, I

just don't think $165 is a lot of money for a pair of socks!" This was at a time when one could get a reliable used car for about the same price. And three tables over, two older women of Jewish descent were arguing rather loudly until one of them said to the other, "Six million of us - how could he have missed you?!"

One time they met Uncle Herald there for an Ansel Adams exhibit. Uncle Herald had been in town giving lectures at the University of Chicago on *The Theology of the Erotic in the Merry Merry Month of May*. Though Uncle Herald's subtlety and timing were lost on him at the time, Ed recalled how as the family and other museumites were viewing some of Adams's most sublime prints in silent awe, Uncle Herald spoke in a mezzo-forte voice, "Gee, this guy was pretty good. Too bad he couldn't afford any colour film." People arched their backs, whispered, and snorted as they walked away while Uncle Herald giggled to himself. That was one of the greatnesses of Uncle Herald - he was the unexpected.

Ed thought that perhaps life moments are the most sincere when they're a surprise. And he thought that maybe it was at the Art Institute that he got his first inclination that life wasn't so much about *Solving* as it was about *Being* - that we're human Beings, not human Doings. So much of life and school had been about completing something to get on to the next thing, about FIXING something. But in this quiet moment of clarity, it struck him that life was more like poetry than math. Even though many forces kept trying to fit it into the math folder, real life always stuck out the sides, spilled past the ends, and bulged in the middle. The silent question always seemed to be, Why do we try and make things different than they were intended to be?

Surely, there had been some grand surprises in Ed's childhood.

While in elementary school, Ed had been fascinated by Daniel Boone, both the historical figure and the TV show with Fess Parker. Whenever the show was on, Ed would dress up in his fringed jacket and moccasins and pretend to fire an old decrepit pellet gun that had been occupying 101 Home Boulevard when they had moved in. The only thing missing from his Boone repertoire was a coonskin hat, which was unavailable in Wedlock and the neighboring bergs. But that didn't deter the folks - Frederick and Martha found one while they were at a conference Frederick was attending in Lacrosse, Wisconsin. During the dinner break they went to some of the local department stores and captured the hat in a toy department for Ed to feel Boonesque.

Frederick and Martha had always been attentive to Ed's enthusiasms, and came up with inventive ways to surprise him. When Ed graduated from the University of Wedlock with his degree in English literature, Frederick and Martha gave him a 1st edition copy of *A Christmas Carol*, signed by Dickens himself. It was Ed's favourite author, and his favourite story. Ed smiled at how immaculately thoughtful that was - a truly tender gesture.

Ed finished his coffee ("always clean your plate") and headed for home. His feet were sore, his legs were tired, and it was 6:10. He went through the front door and yelled, "I'll be right there! Sorry I'm late!" He ran up the stairs two at a time and headed for the bathroom to freshen up. He took off his shirt, turned on the water, and as he waited for it to warm up, he looked in the mirror. He noticed his face - not old, but no longer young. This was his life. It wasn't what it might have been, it was just what it was. This is where he grew up - in this house, with these people, in this town. The connections he had with Wedlock were real. It was home. The people with whom he'd lived his life were not flawless, they were just people with their own bruises from life - their own mistakes that they perhaps regretted but hadn't known how to deal with. Maybe the ceiling had been low in some places, but a part of Ed knew deep in his essence that his time with them had been an opportunity.

How many people got to live in a town with a name that conjured forth sexual themes? How many people got to recount that it was a drunken mayor who'd named the town after racy novels while lusting for a beautiful woman? How many people got to watch a grown man cry at the experience of dobro artistry? How many people got to experience a guy like Kermit Grunder? Ed'd been right about Kermit - he knew that he never really knew him. Ed never knew what it was like to fight in a war and watch your friends become fodder for body bags right before your eyes, day after day after day. Ed didn't know what kind of pain it was to be so far away from a suffering wife, and to then have her die without being able to comfort her. Maybe after so much horror, nothing seems so sacred - certainly not the design of one's transportation.

Maybe much of Ed's formal education experience had been less than he'd hoped for, but it'd certainly enabled him to meet some marvelous people. And amidst all of those contexts, Ed had been able to know the beauty of authentic love with Juliette and Saara. Maybe those relationships hadn't had happy endings, but after all, they hadn't been movies - they'd been real life. Joy and sorrow go hand in hand sometimes, and sorrow didn't need as much attention as Ed had always given it.

Maybe many people in Wedlock were frightened and had

chosen lives of "quiet desperation." Why had he been so unsympathetic about that? Why hadn't he stayed in touch with Frank Sumatra, especially after Frank's wife got sick? Would it have been so much to have at least offered him a call at the holidays? And it was nobody's responsibility but his own to have stayed in touch with Hudson, and Meta. Losing track of them - missing Meta's illness and funeral - those were his own errors, errors that could have been avoided if he'd been thinking about someone other than himself. And Wedlock Lutheran? It was true, the church hadn't often been Church - it had its own ill health, but in the midst of its goofiness, people had helped one another, and many had done so out of the love of God in them. Pastor Scheister? Well, who knows what kind of cruel systems he'd been through. He'd lost his missionary parents at a young age and was raised by loveless relatives in Northern Minnesota. That he'd been left to practice his nothingness hadn't been a good thing, but maybe there was room for compassion even for him.

Uncle Herald seemed to have it - he enjoyed the mystery, had fun with the silly stuff, didn't take everything so seriously, and made the important things the foundation of his living. That was what his friend Stephen hadn't done - he'd taken all of the contrivances to heart until they stopped his.

"Hey, didja fall in up there? Let's eat!" hollered Frederick from the base of the staircase landing.

"OK! I'll be right down!"

Ed was fatigued from all of his insights, memories, and the long walk itself. The jolt of the coffee had waned, and now he just felt spent. They ate dinner, and then the three of them watched two episodes of *Frasier*. While they were watching the shows, Ed took long looks at his parents. Whatever they were or were not, they had chosen to love and provide for him, and had made strong gestures to stay in relationship with him. Ed paid attention to the gratitude that welled up from that understanding.

When the news came on, Ed headed up to bed. As he lay in the darkness of his old room, he felt marathonesquely depleted. And in a very real way, it *had* been a marathon - a marathon of memories that felt like an endurance test of clarity filled with life-offering truths. It had been somewhat painful when he'd noticed them, but now it felt like Light. Ed notioned that it was time to hatch - he could no longer afford to go on being a disquieted egg. He fell asleep with *How You Live is What You Believe* floating through his being.

The morning of life found Ed feeling simultaneously vintage and fresh. It felt miraculous really. The rest of the day was spent running errands with Frederick. This was to be the last day of this visit, so he helped Frederick load the salt blocks into the water softener, and took the lawnmower down to Niewohner's for some new spark plugs and a tune-up. They all took a drive around The Lane as the sun pulled a cover of clouds over its restive rays in the gathering dusk.

Ed's cognition had been through much. His spirit had been through much. He'd gone through something and come out someplace new. He wondered if he'd be able to have the wherewithal to sustain and practice his epiphanies. After all, he'd had a lot of practice rehearsing his insanity. But, he knew he could choose. He wasn't locked into his vacant worldview. He wasn't shackled by the wackiness of Wedlock, or life in general. He knew that he needed to examine his beliefs, for that had been part of the murkiness as well - he had spent so much time on what he wasn't about that he scarcely had any sense of what he was about. Time and practiced awareness would be his friends.

On a Tuesday morning at 8:18, after breakfast with Frederick and Martha, they made plans for his next visit. He loaded his bags into the VW, kissed Frederick and Martha goodbye, and pulled away with a honk and a wave.

If a yawn and smile could occur simultaneously, then that is precisely what the morning was as Ed wove his way out of Wedlock. The day was bright and crisp, the thin cold air making way for clarity. He rounded the curve out by Whylum's farm, motto: *You Can Whip Our Cream, But You Can't Beat Our Milk!* The cows looked up to see who it was that had broken the silence of their entomology study. Ed thought of the Allman Brothers as he looked up at the *Blue Sky*, the softness of the clouds floated Peace above the earth for all who cared to notice, and Ed was noticing. As he drove by Mr. Messerschmidt's place, he honked and smiled. Mr. Messerschmidt was out rubbing down the back window of the Lincoln and appeared as though he was performing a surgical procedure. Mr. Messerschmidt turned, wrinkled his brow, and waved through the morning sunlight. Ed reached for a CD by the Zombies, cued up *Friends of Mine*, looked over his left shoulder just like Mr. Moe had taught him in Drivers Ed., and continuEd.

The Ed

BOOK TWO

Continuing Ed Continued

Ed had some notes:

Clarity is the mindfulness of love

Tainted fruit ripens by its own corruption

If the thing you're seeking does not bring you peace,
it is not the thing you are seeking

The soul does not mark time, it merely records the
uncovering of its essence

Fear is the lineage of ignorance - it is ingrained in us as
anxiety and denial

Plant fear and fear will grow

Religion and scholarship create artificial validity
Civil laws create artificial morality
Advertising creates artificial desires
Self-focus creates suffering

Not about victory and defeat, but about
what one does with either,
winners and losers = conceptual antagonism

Have no interest in the culture's rewards

Avoid accomplishments and acquisitions

Beware power and those who seek it

The way to 'happily-ever-after' is to cease desiring it

Peace lies not in the world,
but in the person who walks its pathway

The meaning of life is the meaning we offer it

Borrowed knowledge is ignorance

Evil cannot be conquered in the world,
it can only be resisted in one's self

Real love seeks no results

The need for certainty murders intuition

Let your heart break, then go on

Riches and structures will fade away, but the integrity
of the intimacy of our relationships will never end

When you think you have "arrived," that you are all "grown-
up" - that is the moment of your death, for there is no more
blossoming once you feel the flower is ripe and plucked

A fact is not the truth

Seek the approval of others and
your heart will never unclench

Seek not to know all of the answers,
but to understand the questions

This went on for thirty-six pages! Ed pondered these sparkles of wisdom he'd been mining in a blurred frenzy of reflection while he pushed up his glasses and rubbed his eyes with both hands. He closed his computer, which spoke *Namaste* upon shutting down. (!)

He'd been trying to engage some of the clarities that had ensued since his first trip back to Wedlock some forty-plus months earlier. He'd made some peace with those early Wedlock years - noticed how some of his frustrations towards the town and its institutions had less to do with them than they did with his own underdevelopments. His appreciations for his boyhood-through-early-manhood had ripened and nuanced, making way for a wiser and happier Ed. But insight and discovery bring their own sets of questions.

Ed spent a lot of good energy on *How You Live is What You Believe* - upon his lips and in his heart. He looked at the ways he'd lived and saw how they were confluent with and opposed to what he thought his worldview was; and he was really trying to dial into what it was he wanted to nurture. Notions are one thing - virtues and truths are only meaningful when they are engaged and translate into behavior; thinking and speaking about them are but whispers of their real place in life. So he'd taken to setting time aside each day for some silence, reflection, and gentleness. Part of this process involved striking up a snail mail routine with Pastor Lebenslieb, which had been illuminating on a host of fronts, and not just a little overwhelming. At times he had moments of, "Be careful what you wish for."

Ed's first letters to Pastor Lebenslieb were queries into "What happened after you left Wedlock?" which were interesting, if not disturbing. Uncle Herald had told Ed, "John Lebenslieb? Oh God. Poor guy." (silence) "That was loathsome, but predictable. What really happened was a mystic meets the law firm of Newton, Kant, and Descartes. Outnumbered, brutalized, disrespected and ignored, he got out of Dodge with only a dozen or so bullet holes shot right through his soul. They tossed him in the moat, sunk his boat, and slit his throat clear through. Damn that was ugly."

After resigning from Wedlock Lutheran, Pastor Lebenslieb had taken some time off from everything but his family, and as the effects of the unhealthy environment receded and spaciousness returned, so did he.

In one of his letters, Pastor Lebenslieb quoted a song that had helped him:

I walked right in the left-brain world
And its fear-based highs
And everywhere I went control-freaks whipped me
'Cause I wouldn't feed illusions with lies

I kinda got confused and drifted from the Muse that loved me
Got blind to the kind of kindness that sets you free
But all the while, something told me -
You could understand

And he could. And he did. He'd written to Ed, "To inhabit an environment that destroys one's spirit is a deep unkindness to one's self. In the moment, it wasn't easy to discern all of the subtle (and not so subtle) harshnesses, contradictions, and socialized depravities, but by clearing some space for me to drop into my heart, they got revealed for what they were, and that needful revelation was its own guide. One takes a few steps back and clarity gets some room to focus."

As a middle-school boy Ed had noted and was intrigued by the way Pastor Lebenslieb had really tried to engage the deep life-truths he'd brought to Ed during that brief year of Confirmation, even if the delivery had been tangential since Ed'd been stuck with Pastor Scheister; but there was something there greater than the concepts - more than intellectual truth - there was something about the embodiment of it all in Pastor Lebenslieb's life that made them different and attractive, refined, even transformed to some deeper thing. Better. And it was this that really invited Ed to invite himself back into Pastor Lebenslieb's life.

In one letter, Ed asked Pastor Lebenslieb how he had started on the path he'd chosen. The response was illuminating: "I always wanted to engage with that which brought peace, authenticity, wholeness, and loving kindness. I wanted to bring the beauty and clarity of the Essence of humanity to the fore, no matter the form or context. Some Calm within said, 'Why bother with anything else? Love is really all there's time for.' Everything else felt vacant and empty. I'd read the story where the Christ figure says 'the sum of the law and the prophets is love,' and if there is truth to that, then the 'savior' is the pathway of love."

And just what does the pathway of love look like? What is love? So often it's used when people really mean affection, or satiated desire, but real love is more complex, and not as "nice" as is culturally implied. And it isn't easy. At least it wasn't for Ed. It was at once clear and not clear, perhaps mostly for the fact that It seemed as though it would require some new wiring, or, more accurately, a scraping of the corrosion off the original wiring, which came by the practice of having the refreshment engage its effectuality.

All of this captivated Ed, but he wasn't so sure of what it all really was or meant, or what specifically to do about it. It seemed true, but he was a little afraid of it; yet, it drew him in and made anything else just seem kind of dumb. And he still wondered, "Why?" But Pastor Lebenslieb's clarities and wisdoms had stirred a shifting in Ed in ways that felt both strange yet familiar. It had been a little difficult to discuss them in letters, but there was so much to ponder - it required reflection; it was the only way one could hope to begin to experience what felt so real and true and good.

He sat back in his natural cherry side chair, looked off toward the cream-curtained window, and tried to recall what one of his earliest "revelations" might have been when he was little. Almost everything then seemed to be somewhat wonderful, all new and "look-at-that!" But one early salient moment came forth.

The family was traveling to Chicago to visit the relatives. It was early afternoon, the sun was up, the sky was blue, it was beautiful *"And so are you, Dear Prudence."* Amidst the tedium, Frederick turned his head slightly towards Ed in the backseat and said, "We're about to cross the Illinois border!" This was a hallmark moment for Ed: any news that confirmed the fact of "we're closer" landed in the "Rejoice!" column. But when they crossed the border, Ed didn't see anything. There was a "Welcome" sign in earth tones with a picture of the shape of Illinois as it might be depicted on a map, along with some reference to Abraham Lincoln in script lettering, but that was all - a big postcard on stilts. Where was the border? Where was that line that was on the map they studied in school? Heck, it was even shown on the welcome sign! But on the ground? Nothing. The grasses were uninterrupted, the fields undisturbed, the tree line untouched - there was nothing to indicate any sort of demarcation at all. Ed looked out the small oval back window of the Bug, left and right - nothing. He was stunned. There was no "border!" It was just pretend! It wasn't a real thing at all! It was only make-believe. Ed slumped back in the seat, bewildered. What does this mean? If there aren't any borders for states, what about countries? Those must be made up as well. So, borders and states and countries were of the family of All-Star Wrestling, only worse because they were taken seriously by seemingly everyone - but Not Really Real! This was a tremendous revelation for a young boy. It was a clarity, but one that initially held sadness, which is often the case with a fallen belief, especially one this significant. The illusion of separation had been revealed.

Hmmm. What does one do with that, especially when even the adults - especially the adults - refer to imaginary things as real? He hadn't been in a hurry to be conclusive, which was a good thing since his initial queries about it went so ignored. When he'd first asked Frederick and Martha, they didn't really explain it too well, owing partially to the fact that it's not really explicable. They said it was just something people did to help organize territories, and keep things separate.

"How come things have to be kept separate?"

"Well, they just do. Do you want some pretzels?" *In Case of Real Moments ...*

None of the aunts or uncles had anything to offer on the subject either. Uncle Herald wasn't around much that summer, and none of the cousins cared, so Ed sort of let it be buried by neglect. But he never forgot it. And he wondered, "What else aren't they telling me ...?"

These were the kinds of things he was hoping to share with Pastor Lebenslieb and Uncle Herald - he figured they were the only ones he knew who might have pondered this stuff, and Ed was increasingly realizing his need for such like-mindedness. It is a lonely place to be misunderstood.

At the recalling of this memory, Ed was beginning to understand that loneliness was also part of what he'd patterned into his life by spending so much time on things that didn't foster intimacy - a lifestyle of thoughts that flourished behaviors that had essentially taken him to loneliness for their sandy foundations of ignorance and flimsy walls of ephemera - work things, money things, material things, technological things; not that there was anything inherently bad about any of them. Indeed, they needed tending to, but not with the primacy the culture encourages. Nope. No thanks. Not anymore.

Maybe it wasn't a good idea to reflect upon these things before bed; Ed needed his strength for his next trip back to Wedlock. Frederick had been slipping even more lately, and he'd been atypically unpredictable - crabby at the drop of a hat - behavior unwelcome by everyone, especially Frederick, once he realized what was happening. "What can I do? My mind is going away and there's nothing I can do about it!"

Ed was looking forward to this visit a bit more for the fact that Uncle Herald was going to be visiting at the same time - just a "summer break" that he said he found himself needing more and more as Wedlock felt so home-like to him. Ed too.

As he readied the car for the trek, Ed thought it might be cool to take his collection of "wisdoms" and post them on the dashboard to refer to on the journey, but once in the car and traveling, his mind drifted elsewhere.

His first thought was the memory of Richard Fenton. Richard was younger than Frederick and Martha and older than Phil. He'd lived with his mom, Werdna Fenton, in Wedlock. Werdna's parents had wanted a boy whom they were planning to name Andrew, so when they had the girl, they kept the name in its transposed form. Rigidity and expectation can be funny sometimes.

Richard was a large man: 6' 4" and about 90 pounds overweight. He carried it well, especially when obesity was nearly in fashion and baggy suits could hide a lot. He sported a highly unsuccessful moustache and had poor taste in shoes, but he was enamoured with Big Band music. He played a little bit of clarinet, and one summer he thought he might want to make a record. He'd been listening to Benny Goodman, Harry James, and Louis Jordan recordings every day, and the joy of those records made him want to do his own.

Mrs. Purselipp's son, Perry, played piano (reading only) and he and Richard had been friends since grade school. Summer was especially slow for both of them, so when Richard proposed they make a record, Perry was keen on it. Richard arranged some of his fav tunes for clarinet and piano, and after a few weeks of practice, they felt ready to record.

Professional recording studios were rare at the time, especially in Iowa, but the University had a radio station with a good enough rig to make something simple, so with a few phone calls they set it up. While deciding on a title, Richard wanted it to be clever (never a good idea): use something about his size and the style of music, along with a hip version of his name, so he decided to call the album "Big Swingin' Dick." Everyone in the family liked it. Few copies were sold, but, theoretically, it made a good gift. In his advancing years, Richard became clinically depressed after he found out Count Basie wasn't a real count. He ended up spending his days watching the same movie, *The Golden Age of Classroom Filmstrips*, and caring for his pet pig, Neal.

This reminded Ed of the story Martha had told about Uncle Herald taking piano lessons as a boy. Ed didn't hear it until his college graduation party, when Martha was ever so slightly oiled. Uncle Herald would routinely complain that his teacher never asked him if he liked the pieces she was assigning, mostly because he didn't like *any* of them, and who wants to participate in music they don't like, let alone learn it? But his disappointments fell on deaf ears - "the teacher knows what's best," which is what most adults said. There was little truth behind it - kind of in the same category as borders.

One time when Herald was assigned a particularly distasteful Bach Two-Part Invention, he was meticulous in organizing the fingering, employing only the middle fingers of each hand, thus tacitly displaying his perspective about his teacher's methodology in general and the music in particular. Of course he was chastised, though not for the subtlety of his gesture, which was lost on the teacher, but because the fingering was 'not the normally accepted fingering for Bach.' Herald, however, thought it the perfect fingering - couldn't have been more apt really. And this was one of those things that warmed Ed towards Uncle Herald; at an early age, he wasn't going to let "normally accepted" conventions warp him, which later helped him navigate the barrage of fear-studded ego-blurred illusions he, like all of us, was to encounter. It's those kinds of early moments and chosen pathways that can keep one clear.

Home-Again, Home-Again

Wedlock was hot when Ed entered the town from the east. It was barely early afternoon and the humidity was approaching Amazonian, the kind of day that would make snakes hang from the trees like flaccid sausage casings. The day was already tired from the brawling heat and the sheer weight of its extremity.

He drove by the old bakery, Smoke'n'Donut (not it's "official" name, but how everyone in Wedlock made reference to it for what really went on there until the "no public smoking" ban went into effect a few years previous). One used to enter the place and see a row of heavy fellows with thick, not-bright-white cups of coffee and same-coloured plates inhabited by two or three large circular and oblong pastries - a Camel or Marlboro in their non-dominant hand - sleepy ancient azure-translucent smoke slow-motioning sensuous northward and horizontal, as though a lens of dreamlike exoticism had veiled the place. It might have been appealing if it wasn't for the scent of death. The space had a strange combination of conviviality and resignation - camaraderie and some faint palour of anguish. Ed had gone there in college and the coffee was courageous and brash, flavoured like the scent of an old chrome-plated ashtray, hot dogs, and just-about-rotting tobacco, in the best blended sense of that trio. Oddly enough, this was a good partner to the oh-so-rich donuts, and the actual experience of the coffee-donut event was filled with pleasure. It was the ten minutes later and the rest of the afternoon that were marked by paroxysms of misanthropy and an absorbing sense of collapse. Ed thought, today? Pass.

It was a bit of a contrast from the inspiration he got from his coffee shop/bakery-of-choice in Oak Park, the Nabalom. He'd go there every Saturday as they almost always had a little band playing against the wall on the left side of the train-car shaped space. Upon entering, one was greeted by the scent of faded photos and a floor of ever-so-worn drunken barn-owl-eye swirls, engraved-by-use into the brown-stone-burgundy linoleum singing with fatigue and character.

A glance around the room revealed an old piano about 40" high that looked like it had been dieting, atop which stood a concave vase of deceased bowed-head pastel roses in dry colors amidst centenarian baby's breath. On the wall behind were hand-painted canvases of clay-toned eagles and falcons – well-suited to that wall, and nowhere else on the planet. The place wasn't beautiful, at least not in any classic sense, but Ed liked it all. It was kind of like Meta's house - down-to-earth. Real. Authentic. It was a co-op, and all of the ingredients in the baked goods were of the highest quality and most youthful of freshness - attentive to the presence of organic and the absence of GMOs, important things to Ed. Made him feel cared for.

But today it was too hot to do much but get to Frederick and Martha's, enjoy the AC, and have some comfort-by-familiarity visits. Ed parked out front, keeping the driveway clear for Frederick and Martha's old cranberry-coloured Sedan DeVille. He switched off the CD player that had been sharing obscure '80s tracks by two bands he'd been having fun with lately - Spank the Nun, and Bees Attack Victor Mature. Frederick was asleep in his chair and Martha was in the kitchen cleaning up from lunch.

Atypically, Frederick didn't awaken when Ed came through the front door, especially unusual for the tremendous lurching squeak that ruptured from the swollen, old-oak door for its pressure against the floor jam. Ed entered the kitchen and Martha looked up.

"Oh! You scared me. Tryin' to give me heart attack?"

"No mom. Good to see you too."

"Well, its good to see you too. Hot enough for ya?"

"Too hot. Feels good in here though."

They kept the place at 67, which when you came in from 98 is a big relief. For about ten minutes. Then you begin to look for a jacket.

"How's dad?"

"About the same ....well, not really. It's worse."

Martha looked like hell. Frederick hadn't been sleeping through the night - he'd taken to a hospital bed they'd moved into the back room supplanting the wicker furniture. He'd wake up confused, in need of something. "YYYOOOO!" would pierce the quiet night space through the monitor Martha kept in their bedroom upstairs. She'd come down to comfort him, or change his Depends, or get him something to eat. They really needed a home health nurse, but had elected not to engage one; and even in his bouts of confusion, Frederick was staunch in his opposition to go to Wedlock's assisted living/retirement home, the Fahrthaus. When originally named, the German population of Wedlock had been just shy of 103 %. Birds whistled with a German accent. Flocks of geese flying in a 'V' formation would switch to the shape of an umlaut while passing overhead. And since 'fahren' means "travel" in German, the name seemed good. Fahrthaus. Its original slogan had been, *"We Care So You Don't Have To,"* which was gratefully abandoned during an effort in the 1970s to "modernize;" the name however was not something open for review.

Ed enquired about some of the neighbors. He asked about Bea Kwyatt, the retired librarian fond of strictness. "Oh, she's fine." 102 and still mowed her own lawn with a motorless push mower she got at Sears in 1963. She had Mr. Edelweiss sharpen the blades twice each season. Mr. Edelweiss had been sharpening knives and blades in Wedlock since WWII. He was still at it.

Ed replied, "I thought I saw her when I drove up. She looks like she could blow away as lightly as mist before sunshine and soft wind."

"Not an ounce of fat on her," was Martha's quip back .

"How's Larry?" Larry Kay, the old cosmetic salesman. Ed remembered being over at Larry and Sherrie's when he was ten, and their son Derry was showing him his dad's antique leaf collection - each leaf carefully pressed between sheets of highly specialized synthetics. Larry had control issues and was watching the show-and-tell, so, naturally, Ed was nervous and dropped one of the specimens. Larry started fuming, "Hey! Be Careful! Whatdaya think, these things grow on trees?!"

When it became fashionable for people to have second homes in nearby Lake Oogie Boogie, Larry thought it'd be better not to take the time and waste the gas on some place so far away - Lake Oogie Boogie was a full ninety minutes distance. What if something happened? So, for a second getaway home he and Sherrie bought a place on the other side of town a little nearer to the river - not so close as to have a view, but close enough to get the benefit of the mosquitos. Frederick had said to Martha, "Well, with that kind of thought, why didn't they just buy the place next door?" To which Martha responded sharply, "Don't say that to Larry! He might do it!" This was probably true.

Ed noticed that between the furnace-like heat and popularity, the old stone birdbath was almost empty. "Hey mom, I'm gonna go out and fill the birdbath."

"Not too full - they just spill it when they rinse their wings."

"Isn't that kind of the point?"

"Just not too full."

There never was much sense in trying to have a conversation with Martha that involved a perspective different from hers. Even when confronted with empirical facts corroborated by credible historical documents, scientific research, and informed experience, it made no difference. One would have thought Ed had learned this by now. But he had not.

He went out the back door, down the steps, under the portico, and out to the old garage. The original doors, which had opened like shutters and latched with a single hook, had been replaced with an automatic rise-and-fall. It was ugly, but it saved Frederick's back, which was needful. They covered the original stucco that matched the house with unpleasant siding when they did the door, but the interior still exhibited the original corner posts which were fashioned from young tree trunks, and, unlike telephone poles, there was nothing to hide the fact that these modest posts had at one time been trees. Ed loved that.

Ed looked at the little patch of ground at the left front exterior portion of the garage where the mint had always grown, and where Martha had always placed the hummingbird feeder filled with translucent raspberry-coloured something. The mint was always special - uniquely-textured and such a flavour. Ed always took a leaf or two off whenever he went outside, and Martha used it when she garnished her homemade lemonade. Good stuff. But now there were just some large conifer bushes that appeared as though they needed to be lanced. The memory was like a quiet wedding of sorrow and delight - an odd grieving mirth.

While looking for the hose, he saw their old Sears push - mower - similar to Bea's, only ever-so-slightly newer. It was the one he'd used to mow a swastika in the lawn, which the folks had made him turn into a cross. Ed had tried to point out that the Nazis had actually co-opted that ancient symbol, which was true enough, but they were right to make him alter it - too much horrific energy around that design to exhibit it in any form, time, or place. The mower hadn't been used in decades except for some rent-free spider condos. It had been in the garage so long, upon entering one could look at it or not, like dirt on a window.

But up on the wall was his old Schwinn 5-Speed Fastback, all black and chrome and glitter-seated. He'd gotten it for his eleventh birthday, and for Ed it was the Bike-of-Bikes. The lines were all symbiotic, the colours the right colour in the right places - they accompanied the form in the way the form imbued it with life. It had style and speed and grace, and it was still here to prove it. Phil had performed various preservation techniques to make it safe to store upon the wall. The chrome was unpitted, the tires flat, the seat unscathed. It was neither fresh nor tired, rather just sort of waiting, like Father Time - asleep. Ed looked at it for a long while, and remembered riding it wearing his orange blast jacket with slim-flaired red-and-yellow trim gracing the zippered pockets and neckline. It kept out the autumn wind when Ed rode down the big hill to school on the frost-singing mornings in thrall to beauty that teared his eyes in the most welcome of ways. He felt good in that jacket - it was neat looking and effective, sturdy and thin, bright and protective. He would play Monkees and Beach Boys music in his mind's ear, slightly bouncing to the groove. Having that as the first movement of the day's symphony made all the difference. That bike took him everywhere and then some, until it went into semi-retirement when Lyle (Doolittle) quit riding his. For some reason, they thought it was "cooler" to walk. By sophomore year the Fastback was rarely allowed to incarnate its title. But it was still here. Ready. Waiting. That was good.

Ed filled the birdbath, completely full. He looked down the back hill of unattended nature - the only slightly cavernous space that preceded The Lane and river - and noticed how its receding hairline was challenging the backyard's edge. A better name for the back hill would have been "the tangle," for amidst the oaks and maples, the ground was labyrinth upon labyrinth of cluelessly ornamental chaos sown in the earth as a deluge of ferns, blackberry bushes, and joyful yellow-toned roses absorbed by a filigree of gently textured shadows scattered across delicate profusions of lily of the valley. It was quiet. Ed listened for the glowing iridescence of the sunlight through the leaves as the heated perfumed earth blushed with luster. Gorgeous.

He looked to his right, behind the garage, and recalled that this was where they had buried Pal, their dog of nearly twenty years. They had welcomed Pal into their home only a little while after Ed had been born. He was black, brown, white and mutt all over, and on more than one occasion, he had been Ed's best bud. Frederick and Martha were both a little tweaky about having an animal in the house - it was never spoken, but there was a little sense of "... it runs in contravention to all polite codes" (reader: utilize a pseudo-falsetto voice with a taut British accent for the previous eight words). So, Pal lived in a little homemade white dog cottage on the front porch filled with old colorless blankets, weather notwithstanding. The only time he got to spend indoors was when it got below zero, or during a thunderstorm - Pal could not abide thunderstorms. He would jump and bark and twist and quake like the torn sails of a sinking ship, in hopes that an Anheiser would understand the tenor of his desperation. And they did.

Sometimes Ed would be in bed pondering the day, then think of Pal and go down and make sure he had enough water. He'd feel guilty about not walking Pal enough, which was accurate. And when they did walk, it was always a major trip, with Pal pulling with everything he had, unable to contain his exuberance, and, maybe, trying to tell Ed, "We need to do this more often, goddammit!"

The first time Ed realized that Pal might be finite was one mid-winter afternoon when they were running on the snowed ice of the river. Pal couldn't keep up. At one point he fell over. Ed had no frame of reference for how to understand this, but he did honor it; they finished the walk with Ed taking Pal's cue for pace. He tried to share some of his concern at home, but only received a "He'll be fine" non-comfort from them. The day he died was the only time in his life Ed ever saw Martha cry. Ed still missed him all these decades later, just like "Mr. Bo Jangles." Impermanence is furiously reliable.

Frederick had come back from his chair nap and he and

Martha were sitting in the back room awaiting Ed. They sat together in their usual places, and there was a great comfort in that familiarity. Ed wasn't sure exactly what it was in the same way one never really knows the moment they fall asleep, but it was something wonderful. They looked out the back window. Laughing aloud, Frederick recalled, "Hey, remember that time Herald 'tended to their garden'?"

"That was pure Herald," replied Martha.

"What?" curioused Ed.

Frederick told the story: "It was a Saturday and Jo (Herald's wife) was asking him if he was going to do anything in the yard. She and Herald had differing views on yard aesthetics, but earlier in the year at a 'family talk' he had agreed to deviate from his Wabi-Sabi philosophy and make things a bit more like Jo had wanted. The garden was a particular point of contention as Herald liked to have the lovely things grow amidst the uninvited natural complexities that enjoyed sharing the space. So after Jo reminded him to 'tend to the yard,' he disappeared/reappeared in the course of about twenty minutes. She found him in his chair looking at a book on the art of Gustav Klimt. 'Done already?' 'Yep.'

"And when she looked out the window he had erected a sign that read: *Boo Radley Memorial Garden.*

"Ha! That was funny!" chimed Frederick slapping his leg.

"I'm not sure Jo thought so ... but maybe," said Martha, smiling.

Frederick continued, "And what was that sign he made to name their house - Jo wouldn't let him put it up - what was that?"

"*Surreal Estate,*" added Martha.

"That's it! Yeah. Ha! That was so great. Herald told me that when Jo saw the sign and understood his intention, she told him his chances of displaying it anywhere were one in a million, and he was pretty sure that was an actual statistic."

"What ever happened to her?" queried Ed. "I only have the vaguest of memories of her from when I was little."

"I'll let your mother tell you about that. I can't do it," said Frederick, as he gently sidestepped the question in nervous silence.

Martha looked at her sandals, then out the window. Ed thought he saw emotion darting in and out of her head like frightened hummingbirds. A part of him sensed she was pleading with mute eloquence, "must we talk of this," as her features tightened ever so slightly with a somber sad solemnity. But there was also the hint of a smile: the kind that belies compassion and appreciation. It was complex.

"She died young. Worn by hardship, genetics, and the insanities of the world, really. Not sure which one of those figured most prominently. I guess that doesn't matter." There was a different tone in Martha's voice - more reflective and compassionate. Clear and sad.

"Go on"

"Well, they had moved a great deal when Herald was first a pastor, and every time he got beat-up, she got beat-up."

"How come he got beat-up?"

"Really? Is that a real question? Herald? His ways in the midst of what was then a pretty rigid institution? His artistic license? I'd have thought by now you'd have learned that institutions hate artists. They hate artists and they hate mystics. They always have and they always will. Oil and water."

Ed understood. Sort of. He thought of Pastor Lebenslieb.

"It was always really difficult for Herald when that happened, but it was even more difficult for Jo. She was too gentle for that much harshness. It got to where she couldn't even work."

"What did she do?"

"Art therapy and private art lessons. Her students loved her."

Frederick chimed in with a tender, measured tone in what sounded like a thoughtfully composed poem, "Who didn't? Her beauty and inventiveness said life was not dreary. She lacked all of the bitterness that animated her elders. Her voice was like the scent of a blossoming flower. She had her moments, like all of us do, but mostly her whole presence was the light of freedom and the colour of love."

Ed could scarcely believe his ears - he'd never heard either of them speak this way of anybody; actually, he'd never heard anyone speak this way of anyone else.

Martha was silent for a moment, then continued, "You should have seen her art. It was like her, like how all real art is like it's creator - it was honest and courageous, simultaneously soft and beautiful. Frederick, what was that way you used to describe it?"

"It had a quality where the thing represented's point of character was in absolute agreement with the manner in which she represented it."

Martha continued, "Add to that 'the depth of one's being', and you've got it. It was as if she could move into her heart, surround it with silence, and let that place touch everything she touched."

They were quiet again, and Ed followed their cue. Then Frederick noted,

"Herald cried for a solid month when she died."

"Then he was pretty quiet for about a year and a-half. If you can believe that," laughed Martha, trying to soften some of the revisited grief. "And then he became a lot like he is now - always right there in 'human.' I think he still cries and he's still quiet, but they no longer define him as they once did."

"I think that's right dear" added Frederick tenderly.

"Did they have any kids? I don't remember any cousins."

"They did - two in fact, a boy and a girl. Their son was an artist like his mom. He was a sweet, sensitive boy. In one of the small towns they lived in, his artistry was interpreted as being gay, which was a pretty big issue back then. And you know how cruel kids can be, especially to an outsider. He'd get physically abused by the bullies ..."

"Goddamn assholes!" muttered Frederick with a justified filth of vituperation.

"Frederick!" chastised Martha.

"Well it's true!"

"One time he got beat up so badly he was in a coma for eighteen months before he died. Their daughter died of SIDS. As a mother, I can tell you - things like that are enough to do anybody in. Resiliency is one thing, but sometimes life can literally be too much. I can't talk about this anymore. It's too sad."

Indeed, it was. Everyone was quiet. The old Mission clock was ticking, but that was it. Though it was delivered as information, the emotionality was pulsing horror and numbness. They all floated in an immensity of mournful silence until Frederick turned to Martha and said, "I didn't wish to be indelicate - I just hadn't thought about that in years; revisiting it surprised me and engaged the old hurt so much."

"I understand" said Martha. "I actually agree with you."

Ed guided the subject ever so gently back to something they could endure. "Isn't Uncle Herald planning on a visit?"

"Yeeess!" said Frederick. "He phoned this morning and said he plans on being here tomorrow some time between breakfast and lunch. He asked if you were here already and was glad to learn you were."

"Cool! I'm looking forward to visiting with him."

"Me too!" said Frederick.

"Well, you'll both get your wishes tomorrow. What sounds good for dinner?"

Ed went upstairs for a little break - it'd been awhile since he just did nothing for an entire afternoon, and it seemed easier here. He slid his right hand across the quarter-sawn oak Arts and Crafts pillars that flanked the wall of the stairway, and remembered sliding down the steps after they'd gotten some new deep-blue carpeting and proceeded to smash to ruin the original antique D'Argental glass globe on Martha's favorite lamp. "I didn't mean to!"

"That doesn't make it any less broken!"

He looked out the window; the summer riverscape was really beautiful. The willows were undulating and the water reflected the trembling of dancing light in a sort of intimate giggling purity. The heat made it seem as though there was an evaporation of colourless, and it all looked heavier. Ed felt a telescoping of time and events he couldn't quite articulate, but he knew it was something.

The "pages of wisdoms" lay atop the meticulously made nineteenth-century almost-black natural-wood dresser with crystal knobs the size of Kennedy half-dollars. He glanced at the

pages. Was anything here connected to anything that had
happened since he got home? The childhood memories as well as
the hearing of Jo's story certainly felt of the family of Real. And
something about them did seem woven with some nuanced sense
of love emanating from some deeper connection with people, life,
and nature - somehow confluent with "The meaning of life is the
meaning we offer it."

"All of this must be meaningful or I wouldn't feel so drawn to
and affected by it," said Ed aloud. Noteworthy.

He moved the bed so he could enjoy the river scene, and let his
mind drift. He started remembering people and wondered what
had happened to them: Alan Rench, the mechanic who had the
first Toyota dealership in town when absolutely no one wanted an
Asian car; Billy Rubin, the neighbor up the hill who loved liver-
and-noodle soup and always spoke in metaphors: " ...went fishin'
and caught trout the size of third graders ... rode hell-fer-leather on
the Gold Wings - got those babies outfitted with everything but
hot'n'cold-runnin' blondes"; Fred "Lucky" Strike, the old guy who
ran the bowling alley and always wore loud shirts, and who once
tried to market a cigarette-themed doll he called Little Baby
Smokes-A-Lot; Sue Veneer, the shallow woman who had the
Useless Trinkets shop downtown; Dick Taiter, the bossy neighbor
who was addicted to french fries; Barry Nekter, the first person to
open a juice bar in Wedlock, who also owned the jelly & jam store,
Currant Events; Greg Fu Young, the fellow who's family had run a
Chinese restaurant in Wedlock until Panda Express pushed them
out, so he started an electric appliance repair business called
Frayed So; Warren Peece, the Russian professor at the University
who truly believed that the quality of a novel was measured first

and foremost by how many pages inhabited the book. And then there was Anna Konda, the woman with the pet snakes, and perpetually dry skin; Debra Kadabra, one of the first female magicians in northeast Iowa, K. Seurat-Seurat, a go-with-the-flow kind of guy who had a connect-the-dots mail-order art supply house; Katena Katelpa - Frederick always thought her name sounded like someone throwing eggs into a swimming pool.

Anne Teetum, the aged mint julep-addicted neighbor up the hill who was still sending out flyers soliciting money for The Widows and Orphans of the Confederacy; Ann Colder, the poison-souled right-wing local radio talk-show host with venom-scented breath who always wore Eau d' Tooth Decay perfume and laughed like Scott Farkus; Dee Spare, the anxious neighbor who thought the couple across the street were transvestites wielding guns.

God! What a fun array of characters! If this wasn't personality, nothing was!

He had the thought to get a bottle of wine for dinner and wondered if The Liquor Store was still in its same spot. Everyone in town referred to it as "The Liquor Store," and had ever since Tommy Heerts and Jim Pussman had taken over. Jim and Tommy had both been employed at the Post Office and were tired of the routine. When the opportunity to sell alcohol to the locals presented itself, they were enthusiastic. While pondering the store's new name they thought it would be clever to use some combination of their surnames; so when the sign went up it availed the first four letters of Jim's last name followed by the first three letters of Tommy's last name followed by "Liquors"- nice and bold neon lettering. Intellectually it made sense, but when you read it aloud .... Ever since day one it was simply referred to as

The Liquor Store. Without asking, Ed thought he'd drive up and see for himself if it was still there, so he hopped in the VW and headed to the edge of town, and indeed, the shop was still open and seemed as it always had. He thought of asking for help as he did in the city, but the selection wasn't as confusing here, so he thought maybe he'd be OK. The clerk was a middle-aged fellow with a bit of gut and a really nice shirt.

"Can I help you with anything?"

Ed hesitated, then said, "Well, actually maybe you could. I'm kind of wanting something light and summery with some butter, eloquence, and tenderness."

"Sounds good. What's your budget?"

"Nothing crazy, but I'm open."

"Try this. It's not expensive and it's one of the best in the store, especially with your description. From France. We got a few cases in last year and it's astonishing really. Hasn't been popular, but I sure don't know why. The wife and I have it at least once a month during the summer, and like I said, it's just what you described. Consistently got 96+ points at some of the big wine vendor gatherings both here and in Europe."

It was clear he knew what he was talking about, so Ed got three bottles and a nice new opener - wasn't sure if Frederick and Martha still had one, as they rarely drank wine.

"Jim and Tommy still own the place?"

The clerk looked surprised that a stranger would know the owners.

"Interesting you'd ask. They sold out to me last year. I'm Otto by the way," he said extending his hand. "Everyone calls me Toot - it's Otto inside out."

Ed took his hand and experienced a just-the-right-solidity grasp. So many people Ed shook hands with tried to squeeze the hell out it, but this was just the right velocity of clench. Ed noticed a little stand availing flyers with a recipe for *Goose Brain Dip*. Toot saw him noticing and said, "It's a Jim and Tommy favorite. Not everybody's cup of tea though."

The Three Anheisers had a very pleasant dinner - fresh white nectarines, cucumbers and onions in a not-too-sweet balsamic vinegar, and a big salad featuring avocados, courtesy of Ed. And the wine. The table was light, visually and texturally varied, and held a purely pleasant ensemble of flavours. Martha offered some ham-swirl ice cream for dessert, but got no takers.

After they were done, Frederick retired to his chair in the front room to watch an episode of *Foyle's War*, so Ed and Martha were left in the back room, and, atypically, Martha stayed seated. Ed asked about some of the neighbors. "How's Jim?" Jim Wilmont had run a duet business providing both tree-trimming services and a state-of-the-art prosthetics retail outlet - called it Jim's Limbs.

"He moved into the Fahrthaus about a year ago."

"Does he like it?"

"When you ask him, he says it's 'fine', but like everyone else we know who's gone there, he'd rather be at home."

"Yeah. Have you and dad ever thought about something like that?"

"You mean moving to the Fahrthaus?"

"Yeah."

"Your father wouldn't hear of it. I think the address alone would be enough to dissuade that possibility. How would you feel sending a letter to a place called 'Fahrthaus'?"

"Well, I wouldn't mind so much if I thought it was a place you and dad felt good about. Just wondered if you were happy."

"Happy? That's not the word I'd use, but I know what you mean, and we're OK. And I mean that. We're OK."

Ed let that settle for slightly under fifteen seconds before continuing, "How is Dad, really. He seemed fine at dinner - maybe a little less animated and a little more reserved, but still himself."

"It's like that. Sometimes it's just a slower version of himself, and other times he has these outbursts that look like some combination of fear and confusion. It doesn't help that he watches that NOX News crap."

"Really?! Dad?! That is NOT like him at all."

"I know. I think somehow the hatred and cruelty animate him, in the worst possible ways."

"NOX. Jesus Christ. Oh, sorry mom."

"No, that's a good visage to invoke if one has been exposed to NOX News. And he's also taken to listening to the local *Ann Colder Show*."

"No! That is SO unlike him!"

"He doesn't even remember them, really. That's what's even weirder. And I wouldn't broach the subject with him if I were you - I've tried. It does nothing."

If anything was atypical of Frederick it was choosing to intersect with those slovenly, hell-drenched examples of media. These brief details made it clear to Ed that Frederick's drifting was strong.

"I do what I can," said Martha. "By the way, Herald called again and he thinks he'll be here about 10 tomorrow morning."

"Does he know about dad?"

"All about it." A few moments of silence and then, "Did you hear we're getting a new pastor?"

"Who's leaving?"

"Nobody, they just decided to add another part-time person. He's not from around here - served at St. Mediocre's in Wisconsin for many years, then half-time at Starbucks Episcopal in the Cities."

"What's his name?"

"Reverend Combover."

Ed went in the front room to sit with Frederick, who was asleep - twenty minutes into *Foyle's War* and already he was out like a light. Ed observed him. He was clearly in a safe and deep rest. It was comforting. He turned off the TV, looked out the big window, and reminisced about the old stories. He remembered the time they had rented the *Lord of the Rings* trilogy and were watching it over Thanksgiving break. During the scene where the Christopher Lee character is preparing for battle and the creatures are birthing from the earth, Uncle Herald paused the DVD and said, "AH! So that's it! That's where the Republican Party came from! Makes total sense now! They always told me it was Lincoln who started it, but this is so much more believable. You learn something every day, doncha?"

Ed thought it was hilarious, but most everyone else did not. Iowa was a blue state, but the Anheisers and their extensions were not fully so. Of course, Herald was neither. Neither was Ed.

He recalled how Herald would be in the front room, reading the paper, and while appearing to look at the "Arts and Entertainment" section he'd say,

"Well look at this ... they've found a new play by Shakespeare."

He'd wait for someone to ask him about it.

"What's it called?"

"Hmmm ... oh here it is, *Lies, Rumors, and Wacky Stunts*," or

"Will you look at this! They now have empirical proof that *The Wizard of Oz* is a documentary," or

"Hey! They found a new opera by Mozart!"

"What's the title?"

"*I've Got Marzipan in My Underpants*," or,

"Here's something we can do today over at the Civic Center in Waterloo: *Schindler's List on Ice*," or

"Hey, the Adult Film Festival is back again this year. At 5:30 they've got the action-packed spy thriller *Lethal Blow*, and at 8:30 they're featuring the aviation sex-film classic, *Cockpit*. Anybody wanna go?"

One of Ed's favourites was Herald's "paraphrasing" of an article from the "Health & Longevity" section: "Well now THIS is interesting. They've discovered that women can actually become physically younger by performing fellatio every day. The effects don't become apparent for two to four years, and the practice needs to be uninterrupted in order for the benefits to remain active, but isn't that something?"

Martha in particular hated that one, "Oh Herald! Must everything be about sex?"

"No, but isn't it great that it can be?"

"Oh brother! You're gonna be a dirty old man."

"What kind of a mind associates sex with dirt!" quipped Herald.

He turned to Ed and said, "Behind every interesting man there is a woman rolling her eyes."

Ed recalled the time Uncle Herald tried to get the premium on his life insurance policy lowered after he'd quit smoking - for thirty-six hours. And the story about when he had a brass plaque engraved and installed on an old worn-out upright piano at one of the churches he was serving: "In the Autumn of 1923, Irving Berlin Pondered Playing a Piano Similar to This One." It was Herald's comment on the seeming need of so many to "commemorate" every material thing, thus making it impossible to ever let it die its natural death.

One time when he called Uncle Herald, the answering machine offered the following options:

Press 1 to leave a message for Herald

2 to speak with a pharmacist

3 for commercial truck loans

4 for image makeovers

5 for the history of quality footwear

6 for spelling reform

and 7 for more options.

HERALDED

Uncle Herald arrived under an instant, early-blue sky a few minutes before ten. The bumper sticker on his car read, *No More Nobel Prizes for Lawn Maintenance*. His vibe was as limber as ever, evidencing a life worn like a loose garment. He came through the door brimming with enthusiasm, the scent of smoked salmon and dark chocolate on his breath. Each of the Anheisers offered him their warmest greetings, but clearly he was the white horse gleaming welcome.

"Great to see all of you! Really - so fun to be here! Missed you guys!"

"Damn your soul, you old coot!" said Frederick. It was a standing joke between Frederick and Herald, as when they were young one of the old guys in Wedlock always greeted his friends with that heart-warming salutation. It was the only time they heard an adult use coarse language without anybody raising an eyebrow.

"Are you hungry? I can make you a sandwich" offered Martha.

"No, no thank you. I had an omelette about an hour ago, though judging by its texture, I think it may have been vulcanized."

They had all visited for awhile when Ed asked Uncle Herald about Pastor Lebenslieb.

"Yes yes, John said you had contacted him - wanted to really know about some real stuff. Good for you. Nice to have an ally in the family," he said, winking.

Martha didn't miss a beat, "Yeah, like you guys are the only ones who care about deep stuff. Just because someone's quiet doesn't mean they're not thinking."

"I know, I know, I'm just messin' with ya. Can't fool me, little sister. You hide it, but it's there."

"It's there for everyone."

"I know. But ya gotta mine it. Talking about it can help."

Martha stood up and went to the kitchen to start another pot of Folgers.

Ed found this brief little exchange significant. It was as though there had been interactions and conversations that had erected a clear and meaningful bond between Martha and Uncle Herald that Ed had never noticed before. In all fairness to Ed, it had been well guarded. Ed knew intimacy made Martha nervous, but he didn't know why.

"What do you want to do this afternoon?" Ed asked of Herald.

"Oh, I don't know. Maybe read a little of the *Tao de Ching*, or a few chapters of *St. John of the Cross*; maybe listen to some early harpsichord music; or maybe you and I could score some angel dust and pick up some skirt."

"Herald!" shocked Martha. Frederick laughed out loud. So did Ed.

"Well, I don't know about anyone else, but I'm gonna watch another episode of my program and take a nap," said Frederick.

Martha added, "I think I'll leave you two to visit. I've got a little grocery shopping to do and then rest before I fix dinner. Anything special you want?" Turning to Herald, a cheery-voiced Martha informed, "Ed got some special wine; we had some last night. You'll like it."

"Great!" sung Herald. "'Curfew shall not ring tonight!'" he said in a thespian-inspired voice, quoting Dickens.

Frederick went to his place, and Martha fulfilled her promise of a schedule, leaving Herald and Ed in the back room with coffee and a basket of the lovely white nectarines. They each reached for one.

"So where's all this enquiry coming from, Ed?" asked Herald in winsome seriousness.

"You know, I'm not really sure. But it's really, really important to me. I started thinking about stuff when I was here awhile back, and one thing I got was about how the way one lives is what they believe."

Herald raised his eyebrows and smiled. "That's a good one. A real truth. How did you come to that conclusion?"

"By looking at my life, my past. What I was doing with it, how I was thinking about it, engaging and not engaging it."

"And ..."

"It just struck me that I could say whatever I wanted, but, you know, being in the garage doesn't make one a car."

Herald smiled at that old joke and its aptness here. "John said you were asking about the nature of love."

"Yes. I really want to understand and incarnate that. Got any ideas?"

"Plenty. Maybe too many. Interestingly enough, prompted by your pen-pal party with John, he and I visited about it as well."

"And ..."

"One of the things we discussed was about how it engages, or how it doesn't. Now understand, I truly believe in love, and it can invite people to transform - it can completely transform. In fact, I don't think one can really develop without it. But like I reminded John, any of our 'loving' won't necessarily change anyone. People change because they make the choice to love, not because you or

I or John change them. Most of the people walked away from the Christ figure. That's the story. One loves because they wish to be loving. Real love seeks no results. True love is actually a very complex thing; and it's simultaneously easy and difficult. Living with that tension brings wisdom, and hence a greater capacity to engage love. That's my experience anyway."

"Like what? What experiences?"

"Tons of 'em."

"LIke what?"

Uncle Herald thought for a quick moment, then asked Ed, "Did your mom ever tell you that we had a great uncle who was a classical organist?"

"No."

"Well, we did. He took me with him on one of his European recital tours - churches and cathedrals all across Europe: Belgium, Holland, Germany, Austria, Sweden, Denmark. We were on the road for six weeks, and while in Frankfurt he told me about when he'd gotten his Fulbright and studied there with the great Bach specialist Helmut Walcha, who was blind. Fulbrights aren't easy to get now, but back then it was a big deal to even be considered for one, let alone receive it.

"Didn't dad have a Fulbright?"

"Yeah - they run in the family," smiled Herald. "Anyway, while we were there he contacted Walcha and asked if we could come by and visit. Walcha remembered him and was happy to have us. We went over there on a late morning, and I can still see it. We were greeted by the housekeeper and Walcha's wife, both with the friendliest of smiles and the gentlest of spirits. We went in the not-very-big living area, which was home to a gorgeous little pipe organ, and there was Walcha, wearing an orange shirt of quality fabric, buttoned up to the very top, neither stiff nor loose - just right. They visited for awhile, in German of course. I got about every third or fifth word - had German since grade school, but book German isn't fast-paced talkin' German. Then Walcha asked if we'd like to hear him play, which we very much did. He began improvising, and your great uncle and I just looked at each other, our mouths slightly open. He played with such eloquence - effortlessly, as though he was smiling or stroking his hair. The sunlight was singing through the multi-paned windows like a hundred close-up teenage candles. It was like the music, transporting us to a better place, or rather, adding a welcome dimension to the present already-good place. God, what a moment! It was simultaneously deep and happy. It was such a generous gift - that whole brief time with him there. He gave each of us a beautifully boxed set of his complete Deutsche Gramophone recordings. Amazing. Then we had lunch in the little garden, and they discussed my hair."

"Your hair?"

"Yeah, I used to have long platinum hair like Mick Ronson."

"Who?"

"Look him up. Anyway, it was over all too quickly, but it's stayed with me strongly ever since."

"What a great story, but ... what's that got to do with love?"

"Everything! That was love. The music was love. The light through the windows was love. Your great-uncle's relationship with Walcha was love. The generousity of Walcha - opening his home, sharing his artistry, giving us beautiful recordings, all of it. Love."

Ed shook his head in agreement. He did understand. Sort of.

"Let me give you another one. I was back in Germany, Berlin, just visiting after I'd finished the first of my graduate degrees. I went into a bar for a late lunch, and I noticed a familiar face at the counter. At first I couldn't place it, but then I did. It was Albert Speer, Hitler's architect turned Minister of Armaments and War Production. It was weird. He'd spent 20 years in prison - I'd read about his release, and that he was publishing a book about the whole Nazi thing. At first I was a little scared. Didn't really want to hang out with an ex-Nazi. But he was just there, all by himself, having a beer. I thought, just for a moment, 'a guy doesn't get an opportunity like this very often ... just see what happens.' I'd always been bewildered by the whole Nazi deal - how could it have happened? How?"

"So, I sit down next to him and start making small talk. He thinks it's kinda cool I'm from America, and I could tell it wasn't his first beer. He's still pretty quiet, kinda reflective; I think he was still off balance for being newly 'free,' which contributed to his enthusiasm for visiting. That, and the beer. I got him going, but he didn't say who he was, and I didn't let on that I knew, which made it easier to talk about the War. He did share that he'd participated in it, but not to what degree. I didn't press it.

"We talked a lot, but essentially it came down to fear, control, unawareness, arrogance, cruelty, sociopathy, savagery, obsession, deprivation, law sharks, horse thieves, egos, money, envy, greed, addiction, aggression, vengeance, criminality, the coupling of high intelligence and boastful ignorance, the monster of passion-without-mercy, and the greatest of these was perhaps hatred - oh, such hatred."

"God!"

"Well, it was pretty disturbing. Even recalling it is."

"So what's the love connection?"

"Its absence! The entire war, like all wars, is essentially about the absence of love! Were love thriving, there'd have been no room for any of it."

They sat there for a minute, then Uncle Herald said, "This doesn't have anything to do with our topic of love, but Speer did have another thing that was actually pretty amusing. He said he had some home movies of Hitler, Goering, Goebbels, and Himmler playing Monopoly at Berchtesgaden. He'd had two more beers by this time and was pretty tipsy, so when he told the story he had to keep stopping to control his laughter. The scene started out with Goering, who says,

"'Nein, mein Fuhrer, you can't put a hotel on Marvin Gardens until you own all three yellows and buy four houses, each!'

"Hitler comes back with, 'But it iz for za Vaterland! I will not be swayed! Now give me za hotel or I'm not playing!!'

"'Jawohl, mein Fuhrer,' and then you can hear him mutter, ' ... but next time I get to be the hat.'

"Hitler stands up and screams, 'It's MY HAT! I can be the HAT any time I WANT!'

"From the next room you hear Hitler's mom yell, 'Oh 'Dolphy, for chrissakes, play nice! It's 'guest's choice!' And be honest - it's not for za Vaterland, it's for YOU!'

"Hitler sits down and pouts while Goering giggles in his green velvet, jewel-encrusted bathrobe, his morphined eyes red like a rat on crack. Then you hear Hitler's mom say to herself, 'I wish he'd taken that class in Buddhism at the Community College, then maybe we wouldn't always have all of this DRAMA! Jeez.'

"It ends with Goering yelling towards the kitchen, 'Ver are za curly fries?'

"Speer laughed all through that, but when it was done you could see he was deeply spent. He excused himself to go to the bathroom, but he never came back. I was kinda glad."

What an experience! Ed sat sort of stunned. The home-movie thing was funny, but the earlier bit was creepy, and he shared that with Herald.

"Yeah, it was creepy. It's a little like the feeling I got when I went into some of the cathedrals over there."

"How so?"

"The churches and cathedrals are startling, architecturally. Some are truly beautiful and offer a really meditative space, and some are over the top. But the real histories of the hows and whys regarding their fruition and whose egos were really being 'honored' is disquieting."

"I never thought of it that way before."

"Neither had I, until I experienced it. Hey, whatdaya say we take a break? I need a little walk and some time to myself."

"Me too," said Ed.

Martha came home and was kitchening, and Frederick was upstairs in the bathroom yelling, "I can't find my special French dental floss! It was right here next to the 4711 cologne! I need it - it's cognac flavored!"

Ed thought about helping, but knew better.

"Oh, here it is. Ha! Right in front of me."

Yep.

At dinner they reminisced a bit. Ed asked about Derwood

Johannsen, who used to whistle with a vibrato like Bert Lahr - you could throw a basketball through that thing. Nobody knew, but Martha, who didn't like not having an answer, said, "I think he might have moved in with his daughter. Or son. I don't know. We didn't get a Christmas card from him this year, but we also didn't get back the one we sent, so I'm assuming he's OK." Making assumptions was a bit of a hobby for Martha.

"How's that VW treatin' ya?" asked Uncle Herald.

"Fine."

"You got somebody good to work on it, or do you take it to the dealer?"

Ed then told them about Juan at Oak Park German Car Repair. Juan had grown up in Ecuador at a time when his family often had to go without food. He came to the United States and began working at a gas station where he learned a little bit about basic car maintenance and repair, mostly on BMWs, which were just starting to become popular at the time. In pretty short order people began requesting him to work on their cars, and with the help of some loyal customers he was able to buy a failing foreign car business and turn it into a thriving one. He was quiet, honest, sharp, and carefully candid ("... an Audi is a good car ... for business"). He told Ed a little bit about what Texaco had done there in Ecuador, and Ed was more livid than Juan. To Ed, the patience with which Juan bore his hardships, and his lack of bitterness towards them, was instructive and inspiring. He'd once loaned Ed a Mercedes when Ed was between jobs. No charge.

"Stuff like that doesn't happen so much anymore," said Herald, "especially in the city."

True.

The conversation took an abrupt turn towards serious when Martha announced to Herald, "Ed was asking about Jo, so I told him about her. Thought he deserved to know since she was such a great addition to our family."

Uncle Herald paused for a moment, smiled, then a few small tears chased themselves down his cheeks in a sacred grief.

"I didn't mean to upset you," said Martha gently.

"No no no, it's OK. The kid should know about the lovely aunt he never knew." He paused for a bit and then said in a very serious tone, "Did I ever tell you about the time I cheated on her?"

Everyone stopped eating and looked at him.

"Maybe it would help if I talked about it," continued Herald. "Life had been a little stressful, and not a little lonesome, and we were at another couple's home - people we knew well and liked a lot. Well ... it was late ... we were playing a board game ..." (the volume and pace of Herald's speech increased rapidly) " ... and ... and ... and I purposely miscounted my steps so I could get the Lollipop Princess card and cross over the Fudge Bars to the Ice Cream Castle and beat everyone at Candyland! OK! There! I said it! And it's nothing I'm proud of! It was just plain cheating, I know! And it wasn't a satisfying victory, I can tell you that! And it's the ONLY time I ever cheated on her!"

"Oh Herald, you really had me going," said Martha shaking her head and pursing her lips.

Frederick was nodding and looking relieved, while Ed was nodding and smiling.

"Hey Ed, is Kiddieland still open there on North Avenue?" asked Frederick.

"No dad. That closed a few years ago."

Kiddieland was Ed's first really cool little amusement park. There was no such thing in Iowa at the time, so when he first went there at the age of five, it was a pretty big deal. It was so colourful, and a manageable size, unlike Riverview which was big and kind of harsh the one time Ed had visited, not too long before it closed. Kiddieland was softer, quieter, roomier. Happier. Ed had gone one last time when he'd learned it was going to become history. They had a sale open to the public - not the big stuff like the carousel, but things like the fun mirrors and much of the signage. Ed chose not to buy anything. He had enough in his mind's eye for all of the memory cues he needed.

Ed cleared the table and washed a few of the dishes while the others continued visiting. When he came back in, Frederick looked tired, and Martha was in an unnecessary hurry to put away the leftovers. Ed asked Uncle Herald if he'd like to take a little walk. Atypically, it had cooled off a bit outside and there was just enough of a breeze to make it hazardous for the bugs. The day seemed grateful that the heat was past, and you could feel it begin to ready for bed. They both changed shoes and took off down the smaller hill towards the Court House.

They walked by the old Hastingberg home, a big white rectilinear place with a tree lawn still home to an old family of maples. One mid-afternoon when youthful Ed was riding his pre-Fastback Stingray home from school, the Hastingberg trees were a torrent of reds, golds, and yellows. The sun was coming both through and upon them with a beauty so uniquely staggering that Ed stopped and decided to "burn this moment into my being," affixing it in his memory by staring at the scene for the longest while, accompanied by the Stone Poneys' song *Train and the*

River playing in his head. Seeing it again, the entire moment came back to Ed as though it'd happened the day before. *"The soul does not mark time ..."*

"Let's walk up this way and see if the Taffeta Catheter is still there," said Uncle Herald. The Taffeta Catheter was the incontinence supply house with a Victorian decor.

"Why do you want to see that place?" asked Ed.

"I used to mow the lawn and rake the leaves back when it was still just a residence. I really liked the people who lived there, Lenore and Ferris Peefenpoof. She always offered me a Pepsi after I'd done whatever it was she'd needed doing - it was the only soda-pop I ever got as a kid. Back then, pop was a luxury. Probably saved my teeth though."

The home looked immaculate. The sign designating the business was rather diminutive, so from the street it just looked like a really cool Victorian. The peony bushes were blooming, and the hydrangeas were voluptuous.

They proceeded downtown and Herald pointed towards a room in a large brick building, "Stayed in there one night - Suite Polly Purebred - it was an Underdog-themed hotel." They both laughed.

"Hey! Look at that. I remember this place," said Herald. "Used to be a deli. Originally it had been the Opera House, though I'm pretty sure there was never an opera of Western European Art Music descent that ever got staged there."

"Then what did they do?"

"It was really like a vaudeville place. That part of it was almost never used anymore when I was a kid. We'd sneak in and just look around. Gorgeous deep-pile satin-and-velvet brocade curtains. The stage was highly figured maple, oiled like the floors in the old hardware stores of the day. Thing was built like a fortress. Loved the vibe."

They stood in front while Uncle Herald reminisced, "The lobby had these handsomely done portraits of men, women, and children - had to be from the early 1900s. Some of the photos had glowing reviews extolling their uniquenesses and brilliances, some of which were likely true. We'd look at them. Closely. Then we'd reflect upon the fact that all of them were dead. We'd make up stories about who probably fought for top billing and better money, which spurred conversations about the desire for fame, material wealth, the need to be admired, the need to get one's way."

"You and your friends talked about that?"

"Well sure."

A few heartbeats later Herald asked, "Remember Fabian?"

"The '50s teen-idol guy?"

"Yeah. The first time he was approached by the machinery that crafted the 'star' thing, he told them he wasn't interested. Then his dad got sick and the family was struggling, so he decided he'd better do something since they needed the money. So often we never really know what people are facing."

Ed thought of Kermit. He thought of a lot of people.

"It's important to be kind, for everyone is fighting a difficult battle," mused Herald.

They walked by what used to be Fineldt's, and Harrison's - homes to the largest toy selections in Wedlock in days long gone. A string of Saturday-morning TV commercial themes started playing in Ed's mind's ear:

Amazing blazing Hot Wheels - they're cool!

Silly Sand, Silly Sand
Nothing else is Silly Sand.

Tutti tutti tutti tutti TOOODD

Tricky Tommy Turtle goes
When your magic whistle blows
Blow your whistle .... he stops!

Six-Finger Six-Finger man alive
How did I ever get along with five?

You can do a lot with Spirotot

It's Give-a-Show
Give-a-Show
With Kenner's Give-a-Show projector

Come to the Honeycomb Hideout

They walked by the old Wedlock Publishing Company, which hadn't been a publishing company since 1931, but the building still advertised the business. That was good. During the '60s it had been the one-vehicle showroom for an American Motors dealership. Ed still remembered one of his favourite cars being parked in the used car lot - a red and white '59 Impala, similar to their old bronze family car, but trippier in the playful colour combination. It sat there all summer and into winter - Ed noticed it every day he walked home from school, and one night after play practice in the frigid edge of twilight beneath the little Valentines-red plastic pennants and low-watt lightbulbs, even half-covered in snow, the car still had an allure. Cool art shuns bleakness.

After they got to the bridge they decided to head back on the other side of the street, walking by what had once been Shoe Biz - the shoe store where Ed got his first pair of penny loafers (terribly stylish at the time). Their colour designation was "Burning Bush," a vibrant chestnut-maroon-reddish brown with a terrific sheen. Ed recalled the dilemma of trying to decide if they'd be cooler with a penny or a dime? He kept enquiring if they'd ever get any Beatle boots in, but they never did; he did however find his P.F. Flyers there.

Music Corner was just gone, captured and murdered by a cruel flood. Ed used to stand in front of the window and marvel at the instruments - teardrop-shaped Vox electric guitars, a black diamond pearl Ludwig drum kit, a gold-sparkle bass with horns styled as flames blazing with a fiery array of anodized buttons and chrome switches. Their visual appeal was its own music.

After they got home, Martha was just finishing up a letter to Gigi. Uncle Herald said, "Hey Martha, did you know that they used to make ink from bat dung?"

"Well I bet that made for a lot of shitty letters," said Martha, laughing and putting her hand to her mouth. "Oh God, Herald, you're rubbing off on me!"

"Good!"

Frederick was asleep in front of *Foyle's War* again. Phil had stopped by and dropped off some stunning tomatoes and brilliant butter-leaf lettuce. Uncle Herald went upstairs to take a quick shower, and Ed sat out on the front porch for a long drink of silence. He always had a desire for calm at the onset of evening.

He wasn't sure he wanted to think anymore, but he couldn't get all of the everythings out of his being. He wasn't agitated, but he wasn't at peace. The memories were rewarding and comforting, but the fact that they were in the past was not. The present moments, and hearing Uncle Herald's stories, were joyful and enlivening, but sometimes they made him feel like he hadn't lived enough and didn't possess enough depth. Part of him felt stuck like a ribbon of film in an old projector, and another part of him had the sense that the confusions on the screen of his life were as much an illusion as light through celluloid. And it was scary when he let himself become so filled with fear that it spilled out of him as "scaredness," especially since he knew how masterfully dumb it was to let those energies flourish. He knew he didn't need to sadden his idealisms and aspirations; he needed to ground and clarify them.

Uncle Herald came out to relay a message from Martha for Ed about evening snacks, and he noticed Ed's pensive state.

"You OK?"

"Yeah, yeah, I'm fine. Kinda. Fun walk."

"Your mom's offering a joyful dessert - nectarines and raspberries, au naturel."

"I'm up for that." And in they went.

After the cheerful fruit-a-thon, Ed kept sending Uncle Herald signals that he wanted to talk more about "real" things, but Uncle Herald wisely said, "Hey, let's get up early and get some coffee and bring it back here - sit on the porch and visit before the day gets hot. Don't tell your mom, she thinks buying coffee-shop coffee is stupid, and she won't be afraid to tell us so. There's a place up by the University with an espresso machine - stopped there just before I arrived here and it was lovely. I made some Gingerjacks before I left home - great old recipe of Jo's with nothin' crappy in 'em. Whatdaya say?"

"I'm in."

"Let the sunrise be your cue to awaken. See you down here then." Uncle Herald left it with, "Thirst was made for water - inquiry for truth."

Ed went on the front porch for a peek at the night sky - the ambered nearly-full moon was at once translucent with energy and opaque with translucence, it was as if its beauty and astonishment foretold the day that preceded it. Like the perfume of ice on a hot day, it was a welcome gift.

The next morning was happily overcast, so between that and the night of heat-respite, the dawn was drenched in a calm of balm and young light. They met on the front porch as planned, drove for the coffee, returned home, broke out the Gingerjacks, and sat together in the alternating lemon and white Tropitone Homecrest chairs Frederick and Martha had gotten from Frederick's nephew who'd owned a patio-furniture store in Peoria. Those chairs sat outside 12 months a year enduring 130-degree mood swings, and after forty years they still looked new.

Uncle Herald began with, "I had a dream last night I was having coffee at a café, and at the next table sat Theo and Vincent Van Gogh. Theo was giving Vincent a book entitled *Follow Your Bliss, the Money Will Come*. I couldn't quite hear what they were saying, but Vincent starts to read it, then looks up as though pondering a passage, and notices how the coffee cup only has one ear. I hear him say, 'Hmmmm …interesting aesthetic.' Theo is looking at the scones trying to find a way to broach the topic of having Vincent become a baker. Over at another table an older woman's talking about founding a Cheerleading Society - it's J.S. Bach's maternal grandmother, Sis Boom Bach.

"Then I'm in my 'dream home' and I'm enveloped in this canvas of terra-cotta, unpainted wood, handmade paper, unpolished tile, gingko and birch trees, pampas grass, ferns, lotus, lilies, red brick, and natural stone. I was so connected to all of them, like they were my friends or something. It was really cool. You ever take a dream course?"

Ed had not.

"Jo took one at the GTU the summer we lived in Berkeley when I was on a National Endowment grant - summer seminar for the History of Love, back in the day when there was money for that sort of exploration."

"How did you get that?"

"Applied. Wrote a good proposal and they got it. Anyway, Jo always said that it was important to trust the feel of the dream, and last night's was really comforting. What a gift."

He continued with his dream sequence, "Then I'm in a church singing *Oh That I Had a Thousand Tongues* and all of these visages of beautiful women were coming forth - women I'd liked to have known in the Biblical sense."

Ed noted, "I have dreams, but I usually forget them."

"Write 'em down if they're powerful; often it's your unconscious offering guidance. Pay attention to that and your life'll be enriched."

Uncle Herald reached for another Gingerjack and took a peek at his coffee, ensuring its needful presence. Ed stared at him for more than a few moments and then asked, "Uncle Herald, how did you get to be like you are?"

"What do you mean?"

"Well, you're so ... developed! You know so much. You embody so much that seems so 'right.' You're so ... interesting! I mean, what kind of a guy studies love?!"

"Well, first of all, thank you for the compliments."

Ed didn't think of them as compliments, really, more just a litany of facts.

"You don't seem like you ever get sad or confused. I know you've had loss and hurt. Do your disappointments and uncertainties never make you frightened, unhappy, bitter, or confused?"

Uncle Herald looked off the porch towards the Shilderstein's hill. Ed could sense he was simultaneously going deeper in and further out.

"Everyone has difficulties in life - it's endemic to being human. Some have more, some less. Different people deal with different things in different ways at different times for different reasons. I've had my moments. After Jo and the kids died I felt like the universe didn't want me to thrive - lost all interest in living really, and that lasted for quite awhile. It softens over time, but not all the time."

After a spacious pause, Uncle Herald continued, "I'm a highly sensitive person, like your dad, and you. And, believe it or not, your mom. That makes things both more difficult, and better."

"You think mom's sensitive?"

"I know so. She's just chosen to hide it, and there are reasons for that - not all good, but real to her nonetheless. We came up in a family system that was pretty wary of intimacy, and therefore it was tragically underdeveloped. And we weren't the only ones. It takes a lot of work to shake that burden-by-vacancy, let me tell you."

"You seem to have done OK," replied Ed, a little surprised.

"Sometimes ... Sometimes. My 'doing OK' has mostly to do with a sense of self-understanding that told me I was either going to have to really dial in to deep, authentic life, or die."

"Really?"

"I know it sounds dramatic, but it wasn't really - not for me. It was just a clear and calm fact."

"What do you mean, 'dialing into deep authentic life'?"

"I can't define it for you or for anybody else, but for me it meant really being able to look at things without the socialized conventions of the over-culture or the distractions and ephemera of poorly focused living that nourishes shallowness, fear, and narcissism. Like everyone else, I'd get distracted by those realms, and I didn't like it. And I didn't want it. And I knew that if I didn't distance myself from them I'd have a life I'd regret. I was not unmoved by the Christ-figure's words, ' ... the kingdom of heaven is within ...' For me that meant that the deepest truest abiding of life is here, now. If I didn't honor it now, then when? I looked at, pondered, and tried to engage that truth, which led me to some clarity about how I wanted to live my life, what was going to 'essence' that. I wanted an honest life characterized by authenticity, freedom, wisdom, generosity, compassion, peace, and love, so I tried to organize my behaviors around those. That felt true to me." Uncle Herald looked downward and concluded, "Kinda simple really. It's basically awareness, intent, and behaviour. But, of course, simple isn't always easy."

They were silent, each reflecting, then Uncle Herald continued, "Growing up and through my first graduate degree, I don't remember anyone ever talking about wisdom. Isn't that weird?"

"Makes me feel lonely," sombered Ed.

"Me too! When I was in graduate school for the theology degree, I got exposed to stuff that helped explain some things - the 'Greeking' of Aramaic mysticism; the dishonoring of experience and intuition - they called it 'The Enlightenment' - Ha! The separation of the soul from the body - when the very word 'spirit' means 'breath!' Saw Constantine turn the Christ figure into a 'conqueror' so he could solidify power. Saw them diminish that cool part of the Christmas story about how we're all pregnant with the seed of God. Once you get a little perspective on how it all unfolded, things become a little clearer, though no less nauseating - an unending pageant of how tainted fruit ripens by its own corruption."

"I once asked one of my college profs why there were backs on the world's sacred texts - did stories of the relationship with the Divine end?"

"What did they say?"

"Nothing really - just sort of stammered and changed the subject."

"A lot of adulthood is about unlearning. No small task. You realize quickly why it's easier to live a shallow life. For awhile."

They were silent, both reflecting upon their deepening

conversation, then Uncle Herald noted, "I saw a little phrase on those sheets on your dresser - something about 'clarity is the mindfulness of love.' That's really good. Did you come up with that?"

"I'm not sure. It was from my notes, some of which are from my reading, some from my journaling."

"No matter - the development is what's meaningful."

They paused, and Herald continued, "It takes a long time. You can't be in too much of a hurry looking for 'results.' Impatience doesn't work. It's sort of like that old unicorn story, you know that?"

"No," said Ed, feeling a little stupid, yet curious.

"That thing where if you go looking for the unicorn, because unicorns possess such a great vibe, it never appears. But if you go about your way fostering all of the authentic and good you were designed for, it'll appear in your peripheral vision. If you turn your head to look at it directly, it's gone."

"So you just keep a healthy focus ..."

"And your yard'll be full of unicorns!"

"Cool."

"Intent and behavior. Imagine if everyone sought one another's highest good, including their own. Would there be any room for the delusions of selfishness, greed, racism, sexism, nationalism? No. Remember all that stuff I told you about with Speer? All of that would have been absent. Can you imagine that?"

Ed started singing John Lennon, "'You may say I'm a dreamer ...'"

Uncle Herald smiled, "Great tune. But I don't think it's a dream. I sense we're each designed with the deepest desire to give, receive, experience, and nourish love. Everyone has their own gifts of enthusiasm and skill that allow that to flourish. How we respond or don't respond to that becomes our life's theme. What we invite into our lives, all that we ingest, becomes part of what we are and what we bring to the world. We are what we nourish."

"Do you think one's environment affects that?"

"Absolutely. Foundationally. A place conducive to peace and wholeness is Peaceful and Whole - it's a big part of love's gesturing, and needful. Do you know that old John Prine song - *Only Love, Love Only, Only Love ...?*"

"I don't."

Uncle Herald looked across the street at the big plate-glass window of Florence and George's and said, "Life on this planet is brief. To live mindfully is important. To love is really all there's time for."

Ed had heard these same last words from Pastor Lebenslieb in the context of their correspondence. Surely it must be a truth worth noting, coming as it did from two of the most credible-to-Ed sources he could imagine. And then he asked Uncle Herald what seemed even to Ed an odd question, but it just kind of came out. "Do you believe in hell?"

Uncle Herald looked at Ed with a soft smile and said, "Hell is just a dark and merciless fantasy of lovelessness. There's no such thing, unless you choose to make it for yourself. Which one can. Wouldn't recommend it. I mean, what kind of Loving-Source-of-All-Life would create something so horrific as a 'hell,' let alone direct one of its beloved creations there? Sometimes I think our biggest problem is the belief that we're separate - from one another, from nature, from the Divine."

Ed asked softly, "When you find your way, even a little, is life gentler?"

"Gentleness is the affirmation of finding your way."

Ed remembered his "borders" epiphany. He was quiet - trying to take everything in.

"Too much?" Uncle Herald asked.

"Yes and no." After a bit, Ed laughed and said, "It kind of reminds me of what Del Paxton said."

"Who's that?"

"He's a character in this movie about a '60s rock band called The Wonders - I think that's the title of the film as well. The drummer is sitting with one of his jazz idols, Del, and Del says, 'keep playin', watch your money - you'll land on your feet'."

"That's pretty good," said Uncle Herald, laughing at the simple pragmatic profundity of the line. "If you have a deep abiding sense of your world view and you engage the behaviours that nourish it and abandon those that don't, you'll be fine; and the bit about the money."

"It sounds so simple. How come it isn't easy?"

"Yeeaaahhh. Isn't that interesting? Another fun Mystery to find a way to be with."

"It doesn't feel fun to me."

"It can be."

They sat in silence for several minutes before Frederick popped his head through the front door - he was wearing light blue pajamas with big white buttons and subtle violet piping. His hair was mussed and his eyes lingered in dreary. In a sleepy voice he asked, "Whatchu guys doin', solvin' all the world's problems?"

"Yep," said Ed.

"Wanna join us?" queried Uncle Herald.

"Uh, sure. Have you seen your mother? I could use some eggs."

"Haven't seen her Dad, we've been out here. Have some coffee. Uncle Herald brought some Jo-recipe Gingerjacks."

"Don't mind if I do!" responded Frederick gratefully. "Hey Herald, remember that speech you gave when they nominated you for bishop?"

"Mmmm ... oh yeah! That was fun."

"I'll say!" laughed Frederick. "... was thinking about that last night - there was a bishop character in *Foyle's War*."

"What was the speech?" asked Ed.

"I'll let your dad tell you. I'm gonna get a quick rinse before Martha gets up," said Uncle Herald, as he popped from the Tropitone.

A smiling Frederick began, "Uncle Herald had gotten nominated for bishop and they were having each candidate speak in front of this big assembly all gathered for the vote. So he's up in front of everyone and starts talking about his 'job reflections' and says, 'For a time I really wanted to be an adult-film star - it was work I had always enjoyed ... but my wife wasn't too keen on the idea.'

"Can you believe it! Ha! Then he says 'I thought I might like being the Sheriff of Nottingham, it's a classic job ... but the commute would have been terrible, and Sherwood Forest real estate prices have always been atrocious ...' Then he says something about opening a cowboy boot factory in Argentina and starting a specialty magazine called *Gay Indian Biker*. He went on like that for twenty minutes!"

"What was the reaction from the people?"

"Some were laughing, but most were not - they were looking at him like he had a drunken pelican on his head. He closed it with, 'And now I'll leave you with a quote by the famous 20-century theologian, Julius Henry Marx '... and east is east and west is west, and if you take cranberries and stew them like applesauce they taste much more like prunes than rhubarb does.' Then he bows, smiles, waves, and leaves the stage! It was great!"

"Did they vote him bishop?"

"Are you kidding? Not a chance, which is precisely what he was hoping for. Remember that old quip by Voltaire? 'God's a comedian playing to an audience that's afraid to laugh.' Herald was never afraid to laugh."

Ed was laughing out loud, and was reminded of the time he got in trouble for thinking quickly in English class with Mrs. DeFun-Gus during his senior year of high school (these were the early days of hyphenated surnames for married couples, not all of which worked). Mrs. DeFun-Gus was usually a pretty cool teacher, but she was having a bad day, and Ed was not. So while he was saying something to Brian Kratchmer that made Brian laugh, Mrs. D. snapped, "Ed Anheiser! Turn around! Now! I'm tired of your shenanigans!"

Without missing a beat, Ed replied, "Really? Well, if you're tired of my shenanigans, perhaps you'd like to try some of my tomfoolery? Or maybe some of my hijinks? If you're really feeling daring I could offer you some of my debauchery?"

While in the principal's office with Mr. Foghorn, who was not known for his sense of humor, Ed tried to wiggle out of it - "She'd been teaching us about how to do creative dialogue; I was merely trying to engage a witticism in confluence with her instruction!" It sort of worked.

Mrs. DeFun-Gus had cooled off by the time Ed had gotten out of Mr. Foghorn's office with three days of before-school detention, which was fine with Ed; it just meant he came in early to a quiet place and got some reading done.

After Uncle Herald was through in the shower, Ed excused himself to take his own. He entered the Rose Bathroom, which is how Frederick and Martha referred to the 2nd-floor bath. They'd ordered some really lovely hand-painted tiles from Austria and the whole room looked like a bouquet of rose-art. It was nice. Ed opened the drawer to the oak bureau in hopes of finding one of Frederick's old electric razors, as Ed had forgotten his charger. There were bottles of English Leather cologne and Aqua Velva aftershave, a slightly-half bottle of Prell, and a clear circular soft-plastic container of large multi-colored, marble-shaped balls filled with bath oil - stuff that had likely been in there for decades. Ed picked them up and looked for the dates; Frederick liked to date his personal products, 'Just to see how long they last.' The English Leather read "Christmas 1971" and the bath oil bombs had "Martha's Birthday - 1967." It was fun stuff to trip upon. No old razor though.

There was a nicked-up blue Matchbox car - Ed flipped it over and read 'Mercury Cougar.' Ed smiled and thought of the time in high school when his friend Dan McCabe bought a light-blue '67 Cougar for $700 - no additional fee assessed for the rust. That same afternoon they drove to nearby Alison to the Dari-Freeze because they'd heard there was a girl there who looked like Linda Ronstadt. She wasn't there that day, and Dan was upset because "we wasted the gas." But is the hope for a glimpse of a beautiful woman ever a waste? Ed didn't think so.

He thought of the other girls in school whose beauty had enriched his life - Serah Clayton, Sandy McCrue, Trish St. Uherstadt. Whatever happened to them? Did their physical beauty transform? Deteriorate? Did their personalities ripen in the good ways they always were? Did they think about the same stuff as Ed?

Hiding at the bottom of the drawer, masquerading as a liner, was an old *Highlights For Children* magazine. Ed slipped it out and thumbed through it. He found the *What's Wrong With This Picture* feature and noticed that there wasn't anything wrong with it at all - it was just more interesting and uniquely juxtaposed than the "normal" one.

Downstairs, Uncle Herald was reading the paper and awaiting Martha's enhanced version of breakfast. He read aloud, "Hey, look at this! Someone found Johnny Appleseed's diary! They've got an entry here; let's see ...

"'Made it to California and think maybe I'm barkin' up the wrong tree. Stopped at a winery on a lovely piece of land just in time for their last tasting and got completely drunk, baffed as a barnacle, looped as a lollygag. It was great! Maybe I should switch to grapes - after all, who's gonna build a chateau and be able to charge twenty-five bucks a glass for some damn cider? No one, that's who. I think I could make some real dough here'"

"Herald!" yelled Martha in a tone of disapproval.

Frederick was chuckling in soft, snuffy tones, and Ed was smiling as he pulled out a chair to the table.

"You a wine-drinker Ed?" queried Herald, "That stuff we had the other night was lovely."

"Once in awhile - not a regular thing. You?"

"I have one glass of wine everyday - of course it's an 84-oz. glass. Right Martha?"

"No comment," was Martha's reproof.

Ed was looking through his "wisdom notes" and thinking about his conversation with Uncle Herald. There was a lot of crossover: love, fear, ignorance, authenticity, delusion, intuition, peace, suffering, meaning. The notes were of the family of truth. Ed's inclinations illuminated them. Herald's stories corroborated them. It was all Real.

He looked into the living room and thought of Christmas time - St. Nicholas Day and the red stockings, the little brass angel chimes that spun from the heat of the candles while their tiny cylinders struck the nickel-sized bells beneath them, the afternoon winter sunlight caress that brought a new deep feeling of joy; peanut clusters, *A Christmas Carol*, snow days, icicles the size of softball bats, gifts under the tree, the fire, Pal in the house. He heard the opening strains of *Where Have All the Flowers Gone* playing in his mind's ear.

His attention went to the table and he thought of all of the times he'd eaten there - pot roast on Sundays, green bean casserole with onions, magical mashed potatoes, Martha's lousy powdered-milk concoction over sugar-laden 40% Bran Flakes, Bugles, braunschweiger. Like the holiday season reminiscences, they were characters to a theme. The theme was the place. It was the people. And it was mixed. Just like the food. Just like the people. Just like life. Just like Ed.

TransitionEd

It was getting to be time to go. Ed had to get back to his routine and "pseudo-home," and Uncle Herald was due to get back to meet his colleague, Pastor Stratocaster from St. Aerosmith's, to collaborate and honor their deadline for a book on a topic he refused to divulge. At first he told them the working title was *Keith Partidge's Hair-Care Tips for Men*, and offered to read them the chapter about the importance of fluffing for half an hour. When the groaning subsided, Uncle Herald smiled and said, "You'll just have to wait - more fun that way."

As he drove home through the hills of Dubuque, the prolific running clouds were making patterns over the undulating hills that for some reason reminded Ed of Jiffy-Pop Popcorn. He thought about something Uncle Herald had said about seeking wisdom, goodness, and beauty that they might be honored everywhere. And something else particularly comforting: "Struggle isn't the pathway to enlightenment, Ed. You already are what you want to become. Your heart is free - engage the courage to follow it."

Yes. Yes.

Just as he was pulling into St. Charles, his cell-phone rang. It was Phil, which was real atypical. Phil never called.

"Hey Phil, what's up?"

Phil's voice was eerily gentle. "Uh. Uh ... dad's ... dad's gone."

"Where did he go?"

"No. He's gone. Gone gone. You know?"

Ed's eyes widened, then his face went into Sadness while

enormous tears formed and bounced off his chest. Right away he felt the presence of leaden, murky, and bleeding. "What happened?"

"Mom went in to check on him after he didn't come out from his morning nap, and she found him more-than-asleep."

Ed had been preparing for something like this, at some point. But how can readiness ever fit into the equation of such a moment? He and Phil visited a bit and then Ed headed back to Wedlock.

There were cars parked out front that were unfamiliar to Ed. Uncle Herald had returned and was sitting with Martha, Phil, and the people who likely owned the cars. Uncle Herald and Phil stood up when Ed came in. Everybody's eyes met and they all started tearing.

"He was so happy!" cried Martha. "He'd had such fun with you two here. He told me he was going to go look at our old wedding photos, and the ones from when you kids were little. I know this sounds stupid, but I just never thought he'd die! I can't imagine him gone!" More deep crying. From everyone.

After the emotion settled for a break from itself, Ed asked, "Where is he?"

"He's still in our bed. I called Corison's (the funeral home). They said they'd be by before 5 - a busy day apparently."

"I want to go see him," said Ed, without thinking. Uncle Herald and Phil both nodded and joined him.

They entered Frederick and Martha's bedroom with the tenderest respect imaginable - quiet, reverent, and in shock. Ed looked at him and stroked his whisping grey hair and said, "Dad," while starting to cry again.

Phil had to turn away and started crying silently with loud bursts of convulsing breath in between each bout. Uncle Herald just stood and cried aloud without reserve. They looked at Frederick. He still looked happy.

Uncle Herald said, "Can I offer a little verbal prayer?"

Ed and Phil said "Sure" at about the same time.

"Give me your hands, guys, and each of you take one of your dad's." He began, "Author of life, we are so sad right now - this passing of Frederick."

They all cried more, then he continued, " ... but we also know that the reason we're so sad is because we loved him so very much."

More tears - louder this time. "We got to be with him for a lot of years, though now it feels far too brief. We know that he's at peace now, deep abiding peace - no more confusion, no more fear about how his deterioration would play out."

He stopped and looked down at the bed, "Frederick, I'm going to miss you more than any words could ever tell. You were the best friend I ever had next to Jo. I can't imagine never hearing you laugh again. 'Damn your soul you old coot.'" They all smile-cried for the shortest of seconds.

"So, here we are in this painful, painful moment, grateful for your life, your love, your ever-blooming gentleness and thoughtfulness, and all of the lovely conversations that brought so much meaning to all of our lives. We understand what death is, and for us here and now it is not welcome and we will need some comfort along this pathway of loss. May we be that for one another. Thank you for sharing your life with us. We now commend you to your Home-of-Homes, a Mystery to us, and

Fulfilled Joy to you. We loved you, Frederick. We still love you. We always will. So Be It."

They all wept long and hard. No way to soften this one. And no reason to. They went downstairs and then each to their own corner. Martha was crying on the phone to someone, and everyone needed some space.

Corison's came when they said they would. Everyone helped and watched and cried as they put Frederick on the stretcher and carried him out to the middle-blue hearse.

"I suppose I should call Gigi. This is gonna be so hard for her," said Martha, crying again.

Frederick loved Gigi as much as the boys, but with her being the only girl and all, his love for Gigi had a slightly different cast - a special quietly-spun hue of tender and spacious. By the time Gigi came along, Frederick and Martha were more seasoned - better parents really, and Gigi was the beneficiary.

The funeral was predictable, a Wedlock Lutheran script. To Ed it seemed more like an ad for orthodox denominational ideology than a helpful ritual of closure. It helped him understand how Lutheranism had been Uncle Herald's circumstance rather than his identity. Reverend Combover performed the ceremony, as Pastor Lurch was visiting relatives in Addams, Alabama, and Pastor Scheister was at the North American Restroom Conference. Yet, strangely, there was a larger peaceful meaning around it, like a halo exuding definitive.

They went to the gravesite - the weather was as comforting as midwestern weather gets, which can be glorious. The sun was bright but not hot, the breeze was gentle and steady, the temperature was warm or cool depending on if you were inhabiting shade or not. Reverend Combover said a few words - their meaning didn't speak much, but his tone of voice did. It was caring. It was present. It was good. It was love.

There was some signal that told everyone it was OK to leave and go back to the church for the reception. Some did, and some didn't. Little quiet-toned conversations started to ripple through the gathering. Phil was silent, fragile-faced, eyes wet and cheeks red. Uncle Herald was simultaneously fully present and somewhere else. You could tell he'd been visited by grief before, and the knowing of it again was stirring the older griefs' terrors. Martha was standing close to the grave and crying like Ed had never experienced before - not in films, not in books, not in real life. It was the crying of Tragic, and it filled the whole space around her. Seeing people in their deepest of sadnesses is not something one can do for very long, especially when they're in their own. Ed was moving between his moment of Loss and observing the others', the latter proving useful as a break from the former.

They rode back to the church in Uncle Herald's car - he and Phil in the backseat, each looking out their respective windows. No one had a voice to speak. Words weren't what anyone needed to hear or share.

Ed was grateful that the reception in the Parish Hall proved to be vastly more meaningful than the service. People from Ed's entire history were there - colleagues of Frederick's, neighbors, old students from different decades, and relatives - some of whom lived nearby but weren't close, and some who lived far away that were much closer. Ed didn't get a chance to visit with them all, but more than enough to fulfill the intention of the event. It helped. Everyone.

"Gigi was heartbroken she couldn't be here," said Martha.

"And so say all of us," replied Ed. "I miss her. I've missed her since the day she left. Is she going to live over there permanently?"

"Well, she told me she's coming home at the end of October, and the duration of that visit is as of yet undetermined. But I'm happy as a bug she only bought a one-way ticket - hopefully that's telling."

"That'd be great!" said Ed. "It always feels more like home when she's around."

"Agreed," said Phil.

Ed went into the kitchen to thank all of the older ladies who'd organized the food. "We do this for all our members," said an early-sixtyish woman who resembled a bespectacled, polyestered sparrow. Ed wasn't sure if this was supposed to make him feel like this was no big deal, or if she was trying to brag. More likely than not, she just wasn't used to compliments.

The reception wound down - the Anheisers and all of the out-of-town relatives went back to the homestead. Everyone was pretty worn out. They sat on the porch and no one said anything meaningful. It seemed odd to Ed that they would have conversations about everything but Frederick, but that's what happened.

When he finally went up to his old room, Ed took off his suit, sat on the bed, listened to the silence, reflected on the day without the ability to do so, and then leaned back, feet on the floor, eyes on the ceiling. The yard light from next door shone upon the ceiling casting long, beautifully-distorted shadows through the window next to the bed. He thought about his dad, the day, and death in general. How interesting that something so unwelcome could be part of every human being's design. It being part of everyone's pathway, why is it so dreaded? Why is it so painful? Ed didn't really dread death, but there was no mistaking its pain today. He remembered something Uncle Herald had said in the prayer, about how "we know what death is," but Ed wasn't so sure he did. He thought about that and about the reason it's so difficult, which was the presence of love. Evidently, deep abiding love has its own facet of pain. That's something. The mystery of death - can one make some peace with that? The presence of love in death's mix - how did that work? Was this one of those times when the questions and answers disappear into one another? As everything bounced around in his mind and soul, Ed fell asleep amidst exhaustion, sadness, over-stimulation, shock, and a deeper sense of how impermanence is furiously reliable.

Next morning's breakfast was characterized by unfamiliarity - the lowness of ebb, the vacuum caused by Frederick's absence, and everyone's inability to make decisions. Mostly they just sat there and shared the occasional thought - Ed, Martha, Uncle Herald, Phil, and Phil's dog Duke, who was perhaps the anchor to that hard rocking boat.

"What am I supposed to do now?" asked Martha.

There was silence, and then Uncle Herald said, "What do you want to do?"

"Nothing."

"Then nothing it should be. If anything, be gentle with your self."

"I'm not very good at that."

"None of us are, but I'm pretty sure it's precisely what we all need."

Heads nodded all around. Duke looked up at everyone, as though affirming their self-discovery.

Ed erupted softly with, "I don't want to re-enter my life. I don't think I can."

Uncle Herald looked at him, "Can you take some time off?"

"Yeah."

"That's good. Do it. How about you Phil?"

"I don't know. Don't feel like goin' back to work - just don't have any oomph."

"That's about right. We're all at the front end of trauma—it takes a lot of energy to navigate that. I'm not planning or not planning anything. Cleared the decks through the end of next week."

Martha cried. Then they all did. Ed looked out the back window at the birdbath - there were seven goldfinches sitting on the smooth-stoned edge, taking turns with little sips, like they were discussing maybe playing cards later that evening. The callow early-morning sunlight heightened their colours and shapes, creating a mood that reflected naturalness and peace. Something about it was comforting. He pointed them out to the others and they all watched the perfect little moment. Frederick would have liked it - he used to get the hugest smile while noting intimate scenes from nature. With good reason. Ed smiled his first smile since they lost him.

No one ever gets over the death of a loved one - they just find ways to be with it. And the one who is lost is never gone from those who are left, they only take on a different place. Frederick was part of everyone he'd touched, and Ed spent a great deal of time reflecting there - the boyhood memories, the adulthood conversations, the insights; just the plain all-powerful joy of two human beings enjoying earthly life together. They'd talked about nourishing intuition in order to engage it, and it did. They'd honored love by never fully defining it in total; they kept the map open and the borders permeable that new revelations might ensue, and they did. All of the joys and connections he'd experienced with his dad were about as life-giving as life gets - the intimacy, the laughter, the shared stories, the reveling in the characters they'd come to know, the literature, the ideas, the art, the music, nature, all of it. For the most part, they'd honored that still small voice inside. And yes, life had its moments of uncertainty and loneliness, but they would pass - frightened energies never last.

A few days after the funeral, Ed had some sense that in time, death's violent ache would diminish; and though unsure of the "how," he decided to let his heart break, and go on.

The days that followed held no form - there was no pattern to any of their lives. Sleep was fitful at best. Food was only slightly inviting. A weighty, throbbing vacant sadness characterized almost everything. All of the things Ed'd been pondering were no longer paramount. His ensuing conversations with Uncle Herald, who was also staying close to the Anheiser fold, were not so philosophical, perhaps because they were in the midst of living an authentic moment instead of talking about one. In some ways, many of Ed's "wisdoms" moved from the inclination column to the "lived." Surely the essence of his soul was unfurling - there was a breadth and boldness that affirmed the fact.

Ed had tripped upon Frederick's last resumé - it was in Frederick's middle drawer in his upstairs office. The education, the published works, the accolades from credible sources, the duties at the colleges and universities - it was all good and true, but when Ed thought of his dad, there wasn't a thing on there that came to mind. Though highly educated, skilled, and seasoned, what Ed remembered was how loving, funny and, well, cute, Frederick had been. Ed thought how odd it was that externally referent adulation could be so appealing, yet so vacuous and substantially inaccurate.

Perhaps things never get settled. Ed realized that part of him wanted to get everything "settled" so his anxiety would abate, but the pathway to "all is well" was about as unsettling as a thing could be. *The way to happily ever after is to cease desiring it.* And maybe all of our expectations of life aren't all that great - maybe it's wise to leave room for "unknown" and sometimes even "unwelcome."

Ed thought about "what's next." He didn't know. He couldn't conjure up anything that made "sense," which made him think that perhaps not everything does or is supposed to. He thought about something Uncle Herald had said - "Abiding nowhere, the heart comes forth." Ed didn't really understand that, but he was drawn to it. He did know he'd been changEd. Amidst everything and not without some trepidation, he was looking forward to being continuEd.

The Ed.

www.ingramcontent.com/pod-product-compliance
Lightning Source LLC
Chambersburg PA
CBHW022010090426
42741CB00007B/973